Theresa Mary (Barney) Forestell
1928 - 2020

PORTLAND - Theresa Mary (Barney) Forestell, died Wednesday, March 11, 2020 on the anniversary of her mother's birth. She was surrounded by her loving family.

She was born to Alfred and Emma (Arsenault) Barney on Jan. 12, 1928 in Portland. She was raised on Lancaster St. and Ray St. in Portland.

She attended Cathedral School through high school. She worked at the A&P Bakery where she met James Forestell. They were married on August 30, 1952 at St. Joseph's Church on Steven's Avenue in Portland. They became members of the Irish American Club and traveled to Ireland multiple times. Theresa worked most of her career with A&P grocery stores. She also worked as a cashier for Cumberland Farms and ITN as a driver for many years.

A devoted Catholic all her life, Theresa was involved in many activities of the church. She taught CCD when her children were young as well as serving as a Eucharistic Minister at Sacred Heart Church in Portland.

Music was always part of Theresa's life. She sang in the church choir from her childhood into her adult life. She was also a member of the Sweet Adelines and she asked him if there was anything he needed, he told her a pillow small enough to fit in his back pack. Theresa and her friend, Pauline, then started sewing and sending "fox hole" pillows to the soldiers overseas. They made thousands of pillows for our soldiers.

Theresa is predeceased by her parents; one brother, Dick, and also a sister-in-law, Marvis.

She is survived by two sons and two daughters, John and his wife Carol of Robersonville N.C., and Paul of Tucson Ariz., Mary and her husband Bill Keith of Gray, and Helen and her husband Todd Stackhouse of Brunswick. She is also survived by two granddaughters and one grandson, Ann and her husband Derek Clifford of Winslow, Kelley Forestell of North Carolina and Joseph Forestell of Auburn. She also has two great-granddaughters, Emma and Elizabeth Clifford. She leaves a sister, Helen Smith of Gorham; and many nieces and nephews, and cousins throughout the States and Canada.

Visiting hours will be held on Tuesday, March 17, from 2 to 4 p.m. and 6 to 8 p.m. at **A.T. Hutchins Funeral Home**, 660 Brighton Avenue in Portland. A Mass of Christian Burial will be celebrated at the Cathedral of the Immaculate Conception

Our Second Childhood On The Internet

Margaret McCue Rogers
and
Theresa Barney Forestell

Copyright © 2012 by Margaret McCue Rogers and Theresa Barney Forestell.

Library of Congress Control Number:	2012901158
ISBN: Hardcover	978-1-4653-9177-3
Softcover	978-1-4653-9176-6
Ebook	978-1-4653-9178-0

All rights reserved. No part of this book may be reproduced or transmitted in any form or by any means, electronic or mechanical, including photocopying, recording, or by any information storage and retrieval system, without permission in writing from the copyright owner.

This book was printed in the United States of America.

To order additional copies of this book, contact:
Xlibris Corporation
1-888-795-4274
www.Xlibris.com
Orders@Xlibris.com
85030

Contents

Introduction 9

The Land of the Leprechauns 12
Saturday, October 7, 2000 13
Sunday, October 8, 2000 14
Monday, October 9, 2000 17
Tuesday, October 10, 2000 19
Wednesday, October 11, 2000 21
Thursday, October 12, 2000 26
Friday, October 13, 2000 29
Saturday, October 14, 2000 37
Sunday, October 15, 2000 41
Monday, October 16, 2000 45
Tuesday, October 17, 2000 48
Wednesday, October 18, 2000 52
Thursday, October 19, 2000 56
Friday, October 20, 2000 60
Saturday, October 21, 2000 63
Sunday, October 22, 2000 66
Monday, October 23, 2000 68
Tuesday, October 24, 2000 70
Wednesday, October 25, 2000 73
Thursday, October 26, 2000 75

NEW ORLEANS JOURNAL 77

Wednesday, June 6, 2001 77
Thursday, June 7, 2001 81
Friday, June 8, 2001 83
Saturday, June 9, 2001 86
Sunday, June 10, 2002 88
Monday, June 11, 2002 94

OKLAHOMA TRIP 97

September 11, 2001 98
Saturday, October 14, 2001 100
Monday, October 15, 2001 102
Tuesday, October 16, 2001 103
Wednesday, October 17, 2001 106
Thursday, October 18, 2001 109
Friday, October 19, 2001 113
Saturday, October 19, 2001 117
Sunday, October 20, 2001 119
Monday, October 21, 2001 123
Tuesday, October 22, 2001 125
Wednesday, October23, 2001 127
Thursday, October 24, 2001 129

THE LAND OF THE GOLF CARTS 131

OUR LIMO RIDE 149

MAINE TRIP 165

OUR INTENTIONS 172

To all the dreamers in the world,
no matter how young they are.

Introduction

One day, at my brother Chuck's urging, I went into a senior citizen chat room. He said, "You should try this." He knew more about computers than I did, so I thought what can it hurt. So, I did.

Theresa Forestell and I met online. She was in the room under the name Thelma95, and I was PeggyM159. Little did we know, when we started talking about things in general, books, and any other things that we could think of that we would form a deep friendship. There were several other people there in the room, but I was impressed with Theresa's friendliness.

We talked for several months. Throughout that time, we learned that she lived in Maine and had a brother in New Orleans, which was not far from my home, in Houma, Louisiana, about fifty miles. She told me and several other chat-room buddies that she was coming to New Orleans to see her brother. This prompted several of us (from the New Orleans area) to say, "Well, let's all meet somewhere."

We arranged to meet at the Treasure Chest Casino for lunch. We both figured that there was safety in numbers, so we brought backup. She brought her brother, Dick, and sister-in-law Marvis. I brought my husband, Roy. I know that we both thought, if I don't like this person, I am bailing out. I'll just have lunch and then say we can't stay. (Sneaky, huh?)

We not only liked each other but also made arrangements to meet the next night at another chat friend's home on the West Bank. Theresa's brother, Dick, sang with a barbershop comedy quartet group, and they had agreed to perform for us.

When we arrived at Doris and Phil's home, there were several other of the chat-room chums there also. We talked for a while; then Dick's group performed for us. What a great group they were. We thoroughly enjoyed them. I took pictures of the group, Theresa, Doris, Phil, Roy, and even managed to get into a few myself. It was a great night. We were thrilled to find out that Doris had fixed a snack for us of sandwiches and Phil had fried some catfish. We really enjoyed ourselves.

When we left there that night, we had hoped to meet the next day. Another of our chat-room chums was coming in from Texas. Well, as fate would have it, she got in late and I didn't get to meet her. I have regretted this ever since. Theresa and Doris did get to meet her. They said that she is as nice as she seems to be in the room. She seems like such a delightful person from the chat room. While Theresa stayed at her brothers, we talked a few more times. We tried to arrange another meeting but just could not work it out. Theresa returned home to Maine, and we continued our online friendship.

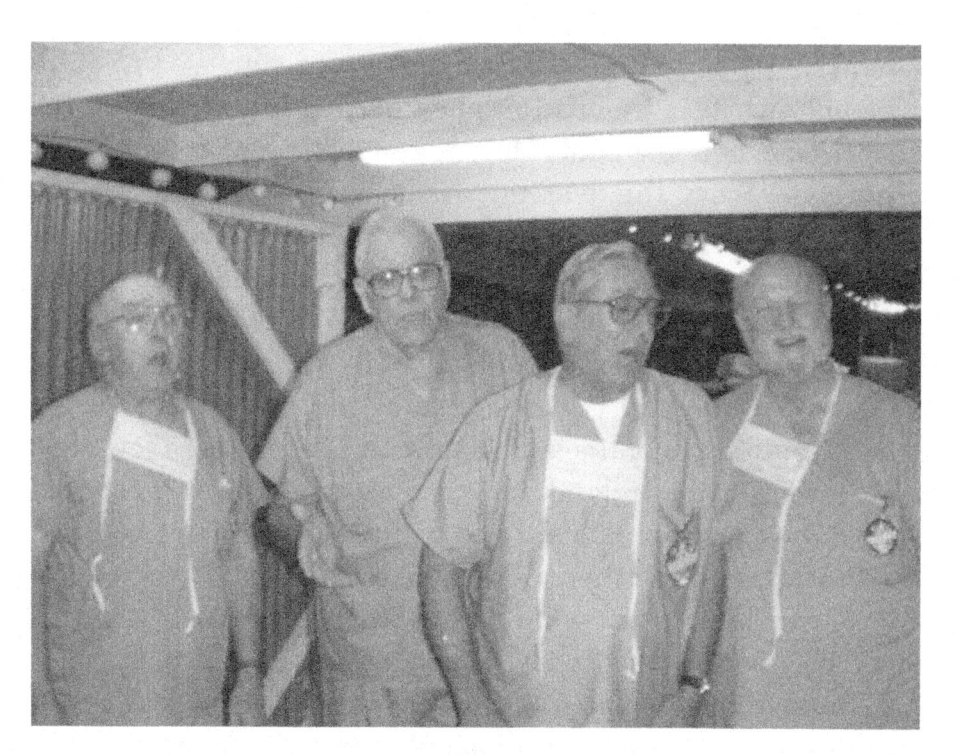

Chords & Aire

The Land of the Leprechauns

One day, I was telling Theresa that I was supposed to go to Ireland with two friends but they backed out on me. I was surprised when she said "Hey, if you still want to go, I'll go with you." Wow, this was my dream vacation. I had always wanted to go to Ireland. My ancestors were from Ireland: I had done a lot of genealogy on them. I really wanted to go. So we decided right then that we were going to Ireland. We tried to talk our friend Doris into going with us but to no avail. So it was us, Theresa and I, we were going to Ireland. We decided that I would fly to Maine and stay with Theresa for a few days before we left for Ireland and that we would rent a car and stay in bed and breakfasts, and we would take our time and do what we wanted when we wanted to. We would stay for two weeks. We figured out what things we wanted to see and not see. Theresa had been to Ireland on a tour about twenty years ago, so she knew what was worthwhile and what was not. I had also talked with a travel agent, and we were getting our bookings through her. She would set up the trip from Boston to Shannon, book the car rental, and get vouchers for the Bed and Breakfasts for us. She also booked our first night at a B&B for us so that we were sure of a place to start. She booked us through Brendan Tours. What follows is the day-by-day account of our trip. Come along and enjoy.

Saturday, October 7, 2000

Roy drove me to the airport to board a plane to go to Portland, Maine. We had a stop in Philly, but it was not long enough to call any of the family to come meet me and have lunch. Oh, I forgot to tell you that I am originally from right outside of Philly. Born and raised in Delaware County.

I arrived in Portland, Maine; I got my luggage and started out the door when a blond lady asked me, "Are you, Peppi?" I told her, "Yes, I am. Who are you"? "I'm Pat, we talk in the chat room all the time. Theresa is outside, with the car, waiting for us."

Before going to Theresa's apartment, we decide to go eat. I can't remember the name of the restaurant, but I must say we had a good meal. It was something like Outback. They had a blooming onion, but they called it something else and I like that, so we ordered one to share. When the meal was over, we went to Theresa's and sat and talked. Soon Pat decide that she had to leave, so we said our good-byes to her and told her we would see her when we returned from Ireland.

Theresa and I talked some more. It is amazing how much we had in common. When we had talked ourselves out, we went to bed. It was nice to lie down. It had been a long day.

Sunday, October 8, 2000

I got up and found the coffeepot. Theresa doesn't drink coffee; that was OK with me. I had brought my own coffee grounds from home. Made coffee and had a cigarette. (Oh, she doesn't smoke either, I'm batting a thousand here.)

After my second cup, Theresa got up and said that there was a Latin Mass at the cathedral in Portland. I wanted to go to that one, so did she. It had been a long time since I had heard the Mass in Latin, and I missed it. We got ready, and off we went.

Theresa introduced me to some of her friends at Mass, Peggy and Kitty Joyce. They told us they wish they were going to Ireland with us. It was wonderful to hear the Mass in Latin again. After Mass, Theresa introduced me to more friends. I must say that she is well liked in her community.

I had noticed a small sandwich shop right across the street from the church when we arrived there. It said that they made Italian hoagies there, and since I love hoagies, I asked Theresa if she minded if we had that for lunch. Being a gracious hostess, she said that was fine with her. So, we got the hoagies. When we got back to Theresa's, we ate and talked some more. We looked at the maps of Ireland that I had brought with me and decided where we would like to go. Theresa had been to

Ireland with her husband Jim, but they were on a guided tour. She said she didn't care for that because they were rushed so much. I was glad that I had gotten the maps from the Irish Tourist Board. They gave us a good idea of distance, but that is what a map is for, isn't it?

Theresa's daughter, Helen, came by, and we talked with her. I had met her in the chat room. It was nice to put a face to a name. We showed her the B&B book and the maps and talked about what we thought we wanted to do. After a few hours, we decided to get something for supper. She and Theresa left and went to pick up something for us. Boy, I sure am eating regular. Shortly after eating, Helen left. I was glad that I had a chance to meet her. Helen was having Throat surgery while we were gone, and Theresa was somewhat concerned about it. Helen wanted her to go on the trip and enjoy it. She was very confident that everything was going to be OK. Her cousin, Tina, was going to stay with her.

Theresa's friend, Bob came by. When he walked in the door, I knew I was in trouble. He smelled the smoke and whispered to her, "She smokes, doesn't she?" When Theresa confirmed this, he said, "Oh, what a shame." Little did he know that I have sharp ears and usually hear everything I am not supposed to. Ask my kids, they hate that. I always heard things I wasn't supposed to, even if they were in their bedrooms with the door closed and the music blaring. Oh well, so what else is new?

Bob stayed for a while to talk; then he left. He was nice, but I will always see him whispering to Theresa, "What a shame." Funny, how you remember things like that so vividly. After Bob left, I pulled out the sofa bed, and we got ready for the night. Of course, we had to have a cup of tea and talk and laugh some more. We even went into the chat room and told everyone hi. Shortly after, I fell asleep; Theresa was still at the computer chatting.

Monday, October 9, 2000

Same routine. I got up and made coffee and smoked. I must say, I am not smoking as much. Theresa doesn't, and she is being so nice about it that I am trying to curb it.

After Theresa got up, we ate breakfast. She told me that she wanted me to meet some of her friends who had been to Ireland several times. She asked me if I minded going there and talking to them about it. You know the pitfalls and all. This was not a problem for me, so off we went.

We arrived at the home of Kay and John Hannigan. I had brought the B&B book and the maps with us. Kay marked some of the places she had stopped at before for us to go. This was good. Now, we have an idea of some good places to stay. Kay told us that we would be fine. (I knew that.) I am a survivor. We really appreciated the advice and their knowledge.

After leaving there, we were going to stop at the Crystal and Craft Shop in Portland to see the owners. Mike and his daughter, Mary Ellen, were friends of Theresa's. She had just returned from Ireland about a month before. These people here sure do go back to the old country, and you can see in their eyes how much they love it. Also, they were selling a CD of Irish music that I wanted after hearing Theresa's copy of it. Anyway, as luck would have it, they were closed, so we did not get to see them. Maybe when we get back, we can see them. We bought some Chinese food and went back to the apartment. We had to make sure everything was all ready. We were leaving the next day.

Theresa's other daughter, Mary, came by to visit with her and to meet me before we left. She couldn't stay long, but it was nice that she stopped by.

Tuesday, October 10, 2000

We just kind of took it real easy today. Theresa had made arrangement for the limo to pick us up in plenty of time to get to the airport, so we didn't have to worry about anything. We knew that it would be a long flight, but we would be flying at night and arriving in Ireland in the morning, so that was good. We both hate to drive at night, and being in a strange country, well, you know how that is. All our plans had been made, and hopefully, we had not forgotten anything. If we did, we will just have to improvise. No problems, we hopped; we could do this and have fun too.

Limo picked us up and drove us to Boston International Airport. Richard, our driver, was very nice. We stopped halfway there for a cigarette break. (This is a curse of mine, I smoke.) He also offered us drinks. I took bottled water, and Theresa had a soft drink.

When we arrived at the airport, we had two wheelchairs waiting for us. We had special treatment. It was great. We told Richard, "Good-bye, see you in two weeks, same place, you have the time we arrive."

The guys that pushed us around were funny, and we laughed a lot. They got us through the boarding process with no problems, and we marveled at how easily it had gone. We had expected a big hassle. What a relief! You just have to know what you were doing, and apparently, these guys did. They deposited us on the plane, and we showed our gratitude. $$$$$

The plane took off on schedule, and we had a nice flight over to Ireland. The crew was courteous and helpful. They served us sandwiches and salads not long after takeoff and then again about 5:00 a.m. they served us tea and biscuits.

Not long into the flight, I heard *phutt*; it was coming from directly in front of me. I looked at Theresa, and she looked at me, and we got the giggles. We arrived at Shannon Airport early, thanks to the guy in front of me. He farted all the way to Ireland.

Ireland trip, country side

Wednesday, October 11, 2000

We begin our big adventure. We arrived in Ireland at 8:00 a.m. I must say that the people on Aer Lingus were very nice; they rode us all around in wheelchairs. They got our luggage and a man to push it on a cart and took us to change some dollars into Irish pounds at the exchange office in the airport.

We decided that Theresa would stay with the luggage and I would go pick up the car and then come back and get her and the luggage. (Sounded like a good plan to me.) So off I went in the little Avis van to get the car.

When the guy at the Avis office brought the car to me, he said "We know all about the dings and dents. Don't worry." And off he goes. I holler, "Wait a minute what about this piece of rubber sticking out from under the front of the hood?" He said, "Oh, we know about that too." So I got into the car and off I went back around the airport road to pick up Theresa. Well, when I got where I left her and the man with our luggage, no Theresa, man, or luggage. So back around I went again. Mind you always driving on the wrong side of the road for me, right side for them. Lo and behold on my second pass, she was there, with the luggage, but no man to help put the luggage in the car. I asked her what happened to him. She says, "I don't know, he just left." I asked, "Did you give him a tip?" "Yes." "Theresa, never tip them till they are finished putting the luggage in the car." After a few minutes of us trying to schlep the luggage into the trunk (oops, boot). A gentleman saw us struggling and he helped us. See there are some good people in this world!

Off we went down the airport road to find our way to Bunratty (where we would spend the night. We already had reservations there.) I had not gone fifty feet when Theresa says, "You're on the wrong side of the road," which I wasn't, so when she saw I wasn't, it was OK. Several times throughout this trip, Theresa would make the same statement to me, and she would be right. It's not easy to change driving habits. A few miles down the road, Theresa told me, "Slow down," I was going a swift twenty miles per hour.

Bunratty was supposed to be right down the road, about twenty miles. Sure! I was driving (doing good, if I do say so myself), trying to read road sign, and it started to rain. I have no idea how to turn on the windshield wipers but finally manage to get them going somewhat but not fully, and I missed part of the last sign, so I say to my copilot, Theresa, "What did that sign say?" She answers, "I don't know." So I say, "You're supposed to be helping me, you're my copilot and navigator, you're supposed to help read the signs." "I didn't see it 'cause I had my eyes closed," she says. I said, "Why?" To which she replied, "'cause, I'm scared." Eyes bulging I say, "What did I do to make you scared? Do you want to drive?' "No, you didn't do anything, it's just the gullies and the bushes, and the road is so narrow. I admit it was a narrow country road with quite a few potholes, but I was only doing twenty, and the bushes were right on the road. It was so narrow when another car approached, you moved as far to the left as you could. The bushes would hit the side of the car when I did this. She was acting like I had a hickory stick after her. She told me that she had had a car accident, and the car had flipped over with all of her children and husband in the car. She said after that, she was always afraid when there were gullies and bushes on the side of the road. After a time, we knew we were on the wrong road. So being a woman, we stopped and asked directions. Well, it seems we had made about a twenty-mile circle and were only ten minutes from our destination. So I came out of the little store to drive the other ten minutes. There was a guy at the gas pumps, just in an all-fired hurry to get in front of us. So I let him. Then, a big truck comes from the other way, and I ended backing up all the way back to the store.

We arrive at Ashford House early. Very early. We were not scheduled to check in till after noon, and it is only 10:30 a.m., and I had to pee. So I went to the door and rang the bell, leaving Theresa in the car.

I was greeted by a wonderful Irish young woman named Shevaun. I told her who we were and asked if we were in the right place. "Aye, you are here," she answered. I asked if I could use the bathroom and said "Oh, by the way, we have reservations." She answered, "Oh no, Peg, I thought you just came to use me lou."

When I came out of the lou, Shevaun said that Theresa and I could wait there if we wanted and our suite would be ready in forty minutes. This sounds great to us, we have been on a plane all night, and we are tired. So, I smoked outside, and Theresa waited inside. Shortly after, our room was ready. We were pleasantly surprised. There was a double bed and a single, plus, of course, a bath. So, we took a nap.

When we got up, we went down the road a couple of miles to Dirty Nellies. It was right across from Bunratty Castle, and we could have supper there. We went at 6:00 p.m. because we didn't want it to be too dark or late when we went back to the room. We told Shevaun before we left that if we weren't back by 9:00 p.m. to build a bonfire to guide us back.

We had a great meal at the pub. I was glad because Theresa had wanted to stop there, her last trip over and they didn't. We tried Guinness Beer. Ugh! Theresa really liked it. So, she ended up drinking both bottles. I am not much of a drinker. I only partake once in a great while.

When we came out of the pub to return to the room, we were greeted with a beautiful rainbow. What a great omen!

Well, the car was boxed in. No problem, I'm driving; Theresa sees this guy and girl coming from their car to go into the pub. So she tells me, "I'll ask this guy to get it out for us." I told her, "Oh ye of little faith, I can do it." She looked at me in disbelief but gets into the car anyway. I backed up a little, went forward a little, backed up again, and went forward, and I made it out. Wee, I am Superwoman!

We made it back with no trouble, except Theresa said I was on the wrong side of the road and I was ready to argue with her until I saw that a car was coming at me and realized she was right. When we got back to the room, we got ready for bed and then laughed half of the night but finally went to sleep. We had a good night rest.

Ireland trip, boat in Galway Bay

Thursday, October 12, 2000

At breakfast, we met three ladies from the States. Kathleen and Shirley were from Colorado, and they were leaving to go south; they were going to be here for ten days; also, we met Janet. She was from Cape Cod area, and she was leaving to go back home later that day. We laughed and talked and had a great conversation along with a wonderful breakfast. We love the Irish breakfast. We could get real used to it real easy. We exchanged e-mail address and promised to get in touch with each other when we returned. They could not get over the fact that Theresa and I had met on the Internet. You hear such horror stories about the Internet that it was great to tell them a good true story.

We had Shavaun make reservations for us at the Finney's in Spiddal, which was just west of Galway. Then, we were on our way.

I was having a hard time adjusting to the road map. It looked like Galway was a far piece to go; to our surprise, it only took us a few hours. It was a beautiful ride. The scenery was wonderful.
We arrived at the Feeneys' in Spiddal, and it was beautiful. This was one of the places that Kate had told us to stay. The house was overlooking Galway Bay. What a sight. Our suite (as the Irish liked to call it) was out of this world. We had a

bay window overlooking the bay, and you could see the Aran Islands and the Cliffs of Moher. We even had a small table with two chairs in front of it so we could have a cup of tea and look at the view. This had to be heaven.

We asked our hosts, Vera and Bart about the tours to Connemara and to the Cliffs of Moher. Vera told us the tour bus company would pick us up at the door and bring us back here after if we wanted. She could arrange this for us with a phone call. We found out later that Vera was the chairman of the Town and Country Homes. This is the association that handles the best B&B's, and that is what we had booked. Aren't we lucky? This seemed wonderful to us. We didn't have to drive; they would pick us up and drop us off here, and the price was only ten pounds. So, we told her to go ahead and arrange it for us for the morning and the other one for the next morning. She was pleased; it meant we would be staying for three nights here.

After we settled in, we asked Vera about a restaurant for supper. She told us about a nice one not far away just a mile of so back, so we decided that we would go there. It was called the Boluisce. It was a small restaurant, but the food and the service were great. As Vera promised, the prices were reasonable. After our meal, we returned to the Feeneys' and read awhile then we went to bed. We had an early morning; we were being picked up in the morning at 8:30, so we had to be ready. We would have breakfast at 7:30. God, I hoped my stomach wouldn't act up.

Ireland trip, Fisherman in Galway Bay

Friday, October 13, 2000

We got up early and had breakfast. Vera told us that she would be leaving to go to an association meeting and would be gone till Sunday. She said not to worry; Bart would take care of us.

The tour bus driver, Martin, arrived on schedule, and off we went. We stopped at the bus barn in Spiddal to pick up a bus. Martin had picked us up in his personal car. When we got to the bus barn, we met PJ, another driver. Then, we boarded a bus to Galway. Theresa had a time getting on the bus because it was high. This was not one of the hydraulic ones that can be lowered. The step was pretty high for her. Martin and PJ got behind her and delicately lifted her from the rear. That was a sight to behold. So you see, we could do most anything we wanted, with a little help and a lift. Hehehe. We had two bus drivers with us. Martin did the Connemera tour, and PJ did the Cliffs of Moher tour. We arrived at the bus office, and then we boarded another bus. (Thank God, this one had the hydraulic lift, so it could be lowered) for Connemera. We were glad that Martin was to be our drive/tour guide. He seemed like a nice person, and we had kidded with him and PJ all the way to Galway.

While we were waiting for them to get the bus ready to board for our tour, we waited outside the bus office. There were several people waiting with us. One man, who was a little ways from us, seemed to be having a problem. He had his fly open. We wondered if anyone was going to bring this to his attention as there were older women there (like us). No one seemed to say anything to him although everyone had noticed.

After a time, PJ was passing me on the sidewalk, so I told him to please see if he could get the man to zip his fly. He told me he would take care of it. I saw him and Peter Lalley (the owner of the tour bus company) talking to the man, but he wasn't zipping his fly. He had a big safety pin at the top of it, and I suppose that the zipper was broken. I had heard him tell people that he was going on the same tour as us, and he seemed to have had a little too much to drink too. Pretty soon, I saw Peter and PJ take the man by the arm and move him to the back. We saw them returning his money. Well, I guess that was the end of that; we didn't see him anymore after that.

We were only on the bus a few minutes when other people started to board the bus. Theresa and I had taken the front left seat so that we could see everything. Martin was driving, and we were on our way to the rail station to pick up some more passengers. It looked like it was going to be a good day, weather wise, and we were glad of this.

Ireland trip, Nuns in Pub, Theresa, Srs, Tessie & me

When we arrived at the rail station, there were people waiting to board our bus. Two nuns got on, so being the fine Irish Catholic girls we were and remembering all the ruler smacks when we were children in a Catholic school (yes, we were both survivors of Catholic schools), we said, "Good morning, sisters." Little did we know that this would seal our fate for the rest of the day.

The tour of Connemara was an all-day tour, so we stopped several times. At our first stop, a pub, we went in to use the restroom and get something to drink. We had gotten a table, and Theresa had gotten my water and her soft drink when we noticed the nuns come in. Well, the only place that was open was at the bar or with us. So being the sweet girls we were, we offered for them to share our table. They were happy to do that. They sat with us, and I told them that I hope my smoking would not offend them. They said no, but I think they were just being polite. Theresa offered to buy them an Irish coffee, but they declined. They got a pot of tea.

During our conversation with them, they told us their names; the older one was Sister Theresa, and she was from Malta. The younger one was Sister Tessa; she was from India. They had only been in Ireland ten days, and someone had given them the rail tickets for the Connemera tour. They were stationed in Dublin at the papal nuncio's office and would be there for a year. We talked with them for a while and even had a picture taken with them. I got their address so that I could send them a copy of the picture, and then I decided to go outside and take some pictures.

Back on the bus, we were off again. Martin was pointing out all the points of interest and playing Irish music. Everyone was enjoying themselves. He stopped on the side of the road and told us that there was a small waterfall about thirty feet back and did any of us want to take pictures. We all were ready to stretch our legs, so we got off the bus. We took pictures of the waterfall and were walking back to the bus when a car pulled up beside us.

The man on the passenger side of the car rolled down the window and asked me, "Is it all right to take pictures here?" Not quite sure what he was saying because he had a Middle Eastern accent, I asked, "What?" He replied, "Does the Irish Government allow you to take pictures here?" Here I was standing on the side of the road with a camera in my hand and this guy asks me if he could take pictures. So I told him. "Sure, the Irish Government lets you take pictures of anything you want." This seems to make him and his companions (four) very happy. Martin was standing outside the door of the bus waiting for me to reboard the bus. When I got to him, he asked, "What did that man want?" I told him, and we both laughed because I gave him permission to take pictures. A few minutes later, we passed the car, and they were taking pictures. Martin told everyone on the bus what had happened, and we all laughed about it because I was as much a tourist as he was.

We arrived at Kylemore Abbey. What a beautiful sight. Now, I understand why my grandmom McCue use to tell me, "Get ye to a nunnery," whenever I got into mischief. She wanted me to live in a palace just like this. Bless her heart. The abbey was built as a wedding present for a man's young bride whom he loved very much. She died early on in the marriage, so he built a chapel on the estate. Later, he donated it to the nuns. What a tribute to her. We took pictures galore.

We went to have lunch in the cafeteria. When we were seated, the nuns were in line, so they came and sat with us for lunch. They had gotten a pot of tea. They had brought sandwiches with them. How smart of them!

When we finished eating, we went to the adjoining gift shop to see what they had to sell. Having found nothing that really interested us, we went outside. We took a few more photos. It was really hard to stop because it was so beautiful. But we did. Then we sat on a bench while waiting to reboard the bus.

While sitting there, we noticed a man carrying boxes into the gift shop. He must have been selling his wares to them. He did this several times. So I called to him and said, "You need a dolley to load your boxes on then, you wouldn't have to make so many trips.' He laughed and said, "Can't afford one." He went on with his toting, and we went on watching.

Ireland trip, Kylemore Abbey

When the salesman came out later, he called to us, "Stay there, ladies, I have something for you." Theresa and I looked at each other in disbelief. What could he possibly have for us? Soon, he walked up to us and handed us each a box, with a jar of body cream in it. He told us his name was Patrick Mulrooney, and he and his family had this business, and he wanted us to have his Seavite cream. It was made from seaweed. We asked him why he was giving this to us. He said, "Because I like Irish American women and because if it were not for the Americans, a lot of Irishmen would have starved and died during the great famine." We took the cream and thanked him for his kindness. This body cream is supposed to smooth out wrinkles. I wonder if he was trying to tell us something. I don't know whenever I have swum in the ocean with seaweed, I always come out all shriveled up.

Martin told us later that it was an expensive cream sold only at high-end shops. We were really impressed. When the tour was over, we passed right in front of the Feeneys', so Martin let us off, which was great. We didn't have to go back into Galway and come back again. He told us he would see us in the morning to pick us up again to go to the Cliffs of Moher tour with PJ.

Around 6:00 p.m. we went to supper, back at the Boluisce. I had the baked brill (fish); the manager (stud muffin) talked me into this. This was new to me but very good. Theresa stuck with her baked salmon.

When we were leaving the restaurant, it was really nasty out. The wind was blowing, and it was raining, thundering, and lightning. I had parked across the street on an incline where some other cars had parked because I thought it would be easier to get out.

Wrong! The car was facing some stores, and I had to put the brake on to keep from rolling into the stores in front of us. Well, I couldn't get the brake off. I tried, Theresa tried, and after about ten minutes of this, I told Theresa, "I'm going to get the stud muffin to come take this brake off." She started to laugh, but I was doing it. When I got out of the car, (in the rain), I noticed the stud muffin standing in the alcove of the restaurant. So trying to save myself some steps, I hollered and motioned to him. "Hey, come here." He waves back at me. Evidently, he doesn't understanding my body English. So I do it again. This time he understands me and, with a surprised look on his face, points to himself and says "Me?" I hollered "Yeah, you, come here," and I pointed my finger at him and then pointed it in front of me. Like I wanted him to come to me. He shrugged his shoulders, and I guess curiosity got the better of him, so he starts across the street. When he gets to me, I grab his arm and tell him that I can't get the brake off, and I want him to do it for me. He looks at me in disbelief and said, "You want me to take the brake off?" I told him yes, and with that, I opened the car door and shoved him in the driver's seat. Now he looks at me with a look like "Oh my god, what is going to happen to me now. These crazy American women have shoved me in their car and they might hit me over the head with their canes and knock me out and take me somewhere and ravage my body." Anyway, he kept his head and released the brake and told me "See, it works. You have to push the button on the end and pull up a little then push down." So Theresa and I both thank him, and I move aside and let him out of the car. Well, when he went to get out of the car, he put the brake back on, so the car wouldn't roll. Well, here we go again, I couldn't get it off again. Theresa and I just sat and laughed for a few minutes, and then, she tried it and got it. Whew!

When we got back to the Feeneys', Bartley was waiting up for us. He was upset. Ten people came in from Philadelphia that he didn't expect, and they wanted breakfast early, and Vera was gone, so he wanted to know if we could take breakfast fifteen minutes earlier in the morning. No problem, we can do that.

Saturday, October 14, 2000

Got up early so we could have breakfast for 7:30 a.m. Went to the breakfast room. (This is a beautiful room. It has a large picture window so that Galway Bay, the Aran Isles, and the Cliffs of Moher can be seen from it.) There is a patio to go out on if the weather permits. It was just beautiful.)

The people from Philadelphia, Pennsylvania, came in and introduced themselves. They were surprised to learn that I came from Chester (which is just outside of Philly.) One of the men worked for the Chester Police Department. They knew a lot of the people and places that I knew. It was very nice meeting them.

We left for the Cliffs of Moher with Martin. We met Peter Lalley (the owner of the bus company) at the bus barn. We boarded the bus and left for Galway to met PJ. (He was to be our driver for this tour.) It was a beautiful day for the tour. People at the bus company couldn't get over how beautiful the weather was for the two days we were on tour.

When we got on the bus with PJ, Theresa and I took the two front seats. I was on one side, Theresa on the other. We were about ready to leave when a young woman asked if she could sit with me. I, of course, said yes. Magdalena came from Mexico but was living and studying in Grenoble, France. She talked to us quite a bit. We enjoyed her company. She was on a rail tour with three other friends and were returning to Dublin that night and would return to Grenoble on Sunday.

The Cliffs of Moher were spectacular. I had never seen anything like them. I took a lot of photos. It was windy there, so we had to be careful where we walked. PJ had warned us not to go too close to the edge. We listened, but a lot of the others did not. We didn't go all the way to the top; it was just too windy and too far for us to climb.

On the way back, we talked and marveled at the scenery. PJ told us that Martin was not only a bus driver/tour guide but also the owner of the pub next to the restaurant that we had frequented. When we got to the rail station, Magdalena reached over and gave us a big hug. We were very touched. We had her e-mail address, so we told her we would e-mail her. (And, we have. We are proud to report that our friend since then has married and is now the mother of a baby boy and is living in Houston, Texas.) How's that for keeping in touch?

When we returned from the tour, we decided that we would go to church in Spittal and then go to Martin's pub and have a sandwich. We had eaten something at lunch so we were not really hungry. We asked Bart what time Mass was, and he told us at 7:00 p.m. This seemed late to us, but what the heck. We could sleep in the morning late then.

We went to the Church a little early. It was beautiful. You don't really expect to see a church like that in a village. Bart neglected to tell us that Mass was said in Gaelic. What a shock, but what an experience. What was funny was, when the priest would talk, it was in Gaelic, and we were suppose to answer in Gaelic, and everyone did, but Theresa, she answered in Latin. I kept my mouth shut for a change. After Mass, we lit candles, Theresa for Helen (she was having surgery in a few days) and me for whatever. We took a few photos of the inside of the church.

After Mass, we went to Martin's pub and had sandwiches, and I had 7UP, Theresa had a Heineken. I looked around for the restroom, didn't see it, so I asked the girl sitting at the next table. (We had seen her and her companion the night before at the restaurant, and she looked like she was local.) After some time of enjoying the music, we decided the crowd was a little too young for us. We decided to go back to the Feeneys'. Good thing we did go back early because, as usual, our big brother, Bart was waiting for us. As usual, we had a time talking about all that had happened to us so far.

Ireland trip, Cliffs of Moher

Ireland trip, Spittal Church

Sunday, October 15, 2000

We met Linda and Al from Chicago at breakfast. We talked, and we were telling them about our car problem when in walked the girl from the pub the night before. She wasn't local; she was from Germany, and her friend was from Germany also. He was a good-looking Nordic god. He didn't speak any English, and we were all laughing about our car story, so she translated for him, and he was rolling on the floor laughing at us.

We asked Bart to make reservations for us at Sligo for the night; we hated to leave, but we had to move on. So much to see, so little time. He made us reservations for Aisling in Sligo; we said our good-byes, and off we went to Knock to see the shrine.

Ireland trip, Our Lady of Knock

We were surprised at how close Knock was to Spittal; it only took about an hour to get there. The shrine and church complex is right on the highway. We couldn't miss it. By the time we got there, it was raining. It rains a lot in Ireland at this time of year. It reminds me of Louisiana. Well, I didn't see a parking place close, so I went down a ways and turned around and came back. Well, lo and behold, there was a car leaving right next to the entrance gate for the shrine. So, I grabbed it. I felt real good about it. There was a priest crossing the street; Theresa told me to ask him when the next Mass was. So I did, and he told me, "At 3:00 p.m." So, I said, "Great." It is only 1:30. We can go to the shrine and then go to Mass again. The priest said, "Oh, you went to Mass already today?" We explained, we had gone the night before, but since we were here, we would go ahead and go again. We told him that we were blessed because we had heard the Latin Mass in Portland, Maine, last Sunday, and then last night, we had heard it in Gaelic at Spittal. I asked him, "What language do they say Mass here?" "Oh, it's in English here," he replied. "I have been coming here for the last three months to help the priest here with confessions, and I must tell you that you are really blessed. Because for those three months, I have looked for a close parking place, and as you can see, I don't have it, but you do!" We thought that was funny, so we all laughed. He left us with a "God bless you." We went to the shrine. We prayed there for a while, got holy water, took some photos, and then went to the church for Mass. Well, the church was packed, and we would have had to stand, and neither of us could do that because we had walked the Stations of the Cross when we did all the other, so we left.

We walked across the street to a tearoom, and there was a souvenir shop connected to it. It was rainy and cold, so we decided to have a pot of tea and a sandwich before getting our souvenirs and going on to Sligo.

Ireland trip, Our Lady of Knock

When we walked in the tearoom, a man sitting at a table said, "There's the lady from Louisiana," and a woman said, "Hello, Theresa." It was the people from Philly. We talked with them for a few minutes, marveling about how small the world was and asked where they were headed for next. We used the restroom, came back to the table, and ordered. After we ate, we went to the shop next door and bought our souvenirs. Then, we left for Sligo.

Theresa claims that when I pulled out of the parking place, I banged the rearview mirror on the door of the car in front of me. So I stopped and checked. I didn't see anything wrong with it or with mine. So I chalked it up to Theresa having a senior moment and went on. We passed the Philly group on the way out of town, so we blew the horn at them. They all waved. What a surprise that was!

Sligo was only about an hour and a half away; we were in good shape. When we arrived at Aisling, the home of Des and Nan Faul, we were greeted by their son, Des Junior. He was a nice-looking young man, and he explained that his parents were gone but would be back later, and we would meet them for breakfast in the morning. He helped us with the bags, and then he brought us tea and cakes. He told me that we could make a call to the United States from there. Just to let him know when we were ready. The room was small, but we decided to grin and bear it. It was only for one night, and it did have the double and single bed we had become accustomed to and a small bathroom.

About an hour later, I went to make a call to Roy. Des Junior was not there; I met his younger brother. He was a looker too. I figured Roy would be home at this time because it was 8:00 p.m. in Ireland, so it was 3:00 p.m. on Sunday. He would be sitting in front of the TV watching his beloved Saints. He was. We talked for a few minutes; he was pleased to tell me that everything at home was fine. Complained about the heat and that a piece on the tractor had broken yesterday, and he would need to go tomorrow to see if he could find a piece like that. After our good-bye, I went outside to smoke a cigarette. Every place we had stopped so far had a no-smoking house, so I had to go outside to smoke. I was doing great. Wasn't smoking much at all.

Monday, October 16, 2000

We had breakfast and met the parents of the two young studs. We met a couple from Australia also. After, we had Des Fail make a reservation for us in Donegal, and off we were again.

Theresa had been all ready for Donegal. She had been there before and said that she loved the town and the shops, so we could do some shopping there.

It took us a while, but we found the Millhouse run by Bernie Malherne. The room was a nice size. We asked about a place to eat supper, and she recommended Harbor House in town. We also asked her where we could change some money. She told us the bank in town but that we needed to go soon because it closed at 4:00 p.m. So off we went again.

We made it just in time for the bank. Good thing I got a nice parking place close to the center of town, so we started our shopping. Theresa wanted a hat. So, we started looking for one. We couldn't find one in the store we were that she liked. Have you ever had the feeling that someone is staring at you? Well, I did. It was a woman around our age; her name was Mary B. Chippings. Finally, she asked me if I had bought my shawl there and in what department because she wanted one like it. Theresa told her that I had made it and that we were from the States. As you would have it, she was on the tourist board there, just as I was in Louisiana, and she was also a constable. We talked for a while, and she advised us where to look for souvenirs we wanted to buy to take back for the kids. She also reaffirmed that the Harbor House was a great place to eat. She also got out in the middle of the street and stopped traffic so Theresa and I could cross safely. (Wish I had taken a photo of her, hindsight is a wonderful thing.) She was a delightful lady.

We did our shopping. Finding more than we had come for. We found out from the shopgirl that I had parked in a place that I need a special card for and I would probably get a ticket. Well, how was I to know? So, I went to the car and put all our purchases in the trunk. Guess what? Lucky me, no ticket! Theresa waited for me at the shop. She was very tired. I didn't want her to have to walk too much, and she was already tired from the shopping. I drove to the Harbor House, and we got to park legally across the street from it. We had a very good meal, and then we went back to the B&B at about 8:15 p.m.

When we got back to the Millhouse, we wanted to take our purchases in with us, and look at them. (You know how women are!) Well, I couldn't get the trunk open. I tried and I tried. I had opened it to put them in, why couldn't I open it to get them out? So Mr. Malherne helped me to open it. (It was embarrassing.) Anyway, we looked at everything and then put them in our suitcases. We had not filled our suitcases on the way over here, so we had some room to play with. After all of this, I was tired and wanted a shower. Well, it's a good thing I checked to see if I had everything I needed because there were no face rags in there. So, I went to find Bernie. She was very surprised when I told her that I needed face rags for us. She told Theresa and I that she never provides face rags for her guest because face rags are *personal items*. (Are you kidding me?) "Most people, she told us, have their own." She has never even been asked for one before. If we wanted, she will bring us two more small towels that we can use. So we told her to bring them. We had a good laugh on that one. Imagine, face rags are personal items.

I must say that the room was large with a very nice bath, and the people were very friendly. Bernie had five children, and we never heard them. She had one in diapers and one just barely walking. The rest were in school. Irish sure believe in large families.

Tuesday, October 17, 2000

Theresa and I had a good breakfast, and then we asked Bertie to make reservations for us in Mulligar. It took several calls because some of the B&B's had closed for the season. When she did get us a reservation, she was worried about it because it was an upstairs bedroom and Bertie knew that we would have trouble because we both walked with canes. However, the man, Mr. Healy, assured her that they were very gentle steps. (I have never heard of stairs being called "gentle steps." He assured her that it would not be hard on us as he had had heart surgery a month earlier and he was able to maneuver them very well. So she asked us if we wanted to take this room. So we told her sure, if he thought it would not be too hard for us. (We wanted to see what gentle steps look like.) Theresa held Bertie's baby the whole time she was on the phone, and I talked with the toddler, Jack. He was so cute. She was very nice to us. But then, everyone had been very nice to us since we left the airport. (That porter stiffed us.)

When we left for Mulligar, it was windy and rainy and cold. It would take us four hours to get to Glenmore House. The home of Mr. and Mrs. Healy. We took our time because of the weather. We had a good highway to travel on though. We stopped and got gas and had a pot of tea about midway.

When we arrived at Glenmore House, we were shocked. It was a beautiful Georgian manor house. It was just like a palace. When Mr. Healy opened the door, he turned out to be a very distinguished-looking gentleman in his late sixties or early seventies.

He offered us a pot of tea, which we gladly accepted. Then, he led us to the breakfast room. You should have seen this room. It belonged in this house. It was fabulous. The china on the table was Prince Albert. We felt like we were in a fairy tale. We asked him about supper. If there was a place that would deliver to us. He told us no, but he would be happy to go get us something later if we liked. We were very happy about this. He had menus from several places, so we picked the Chinese and paid him for it. Then he told us to leave our luggage, that someone would bring it up later for us.

He led us to the stairs (the gentle ones), and I thought I'd never make it. It looked like it was so far up there. He took Theresa's tote bag and carried it up the stairs for her. Nice man. Well, on the way up the stairs, he was about three steps in front of me, and Theresa was about three steps behind me; all of a sudden, we heard *phuttt* Sounded like a fart. Oh no, the plane ride all over again. Mr. Healy set Theresa's bag down, and then, he turned around and looked at me. I turned and looked at Theresa. Then, he picked up her bag and started up the stairs again. All of a sudden, I heard *phutt* again in front of me. I wanted to burst out laughing, but he was such a distinguished-looking man, I couldn't. He set the bag down on the steps again; he looked at both of us with wonder, and then he picked it up again and started back up the stairs. Theresa and I were about to roll on down the gentle steps because we were trying not to laugh, when all of a sudden, we heard *phutt* again. He set down the bag and looked at Theresa and said, "What do you have in this bag that keeps going off?" Theresa answered him, "Nothing." He looked at us like we were from the IRA, and we had come to bomb his house. Theresa assured him that there was nothing in her bag that could be going off. I told him, "She doesn't even have a hair dryer in there." So, he picked up the bag again, and then I heard a whirling sound. *Whrrr*. Then it hit me. I knew what it was! I turned around and told Theresa, "It's your little portable handheld fan. It's going off!" He looked at both of us like we had both lost our minds. We tried to explain it to him, but he was having none of it. So I told Theresa that as soon as we get to the room, she was going to have to show it to him. Well, I don't think he believed us; when we got to the room, she opened the bag and showed him the fan. He said he would see us later when he brought us our Chinese food, and he left. Theresa and I fell out laughing. We laughed so hard we cried.

Later, his wife, Regina (she seemed to be about thirty years younger than him, very pretty, she reminded me of Jackie Kennedy Onassis) knocked on the door and told us that our bags were there and wanted to know if we needed anything. We talked to her for a while; she asked us about the fan. She said she would like to see it. So, Theresa showed it to her. There was nothing unusual about this fan; you see them all over. Especially at amusement parks. People walking around with the fan to their faces, trying to cool down.

That evening, Regina returned with our Chinese food. We thanked her and told her how much we appreciated them for getting it for us. We could not have climbed those gentle steps again. We did not see Mr. Healy again during our stay there. I guess we had scared him off. Hehehe. After eating, I took my shower. Then I read for a while and went to sleep. Theresa was going to take a shower, but the bathroom and the shower were very small, and she started to get claustrophobic. It really was very small, but she managed to get through it. Then she watched TV.

Wednesday, October 18, 2000

Ireland trip, Castle Ruins

Theresa and I had a very nice breakfast. The table and the place settings were beautiful. I took a few photos of it. Then we ate. Regina told us she would be leaving soon as she had a golf date and that her husband was out. But not to worry that if we needed anything, Mary, the maid, would be there to help us. We asked her if she could make reservations for us outside of Kilkenny, at Hartford House in Kilmandgh. She did. She talked to us awhile and then she left. Pip, the dog, came in and kept us company. Mary was very nice. She talked to us for a while too. She gave us directions to Kilkenny. We were going to have a long ride today, mostly back roads, but they were well marked. So, we didn't have any trouble.

It took us four hours to get to Kilmandgh, just outside of Callan and Kilkenny. We had a time finding Hartford House, but we did find it. Oh, ye of little faith. We had wanted to stay there because it advertised traditional music in the B&B book.

When we got to Hartford House, we were greeted by the family dog. Now you would have to see this dog. He was bigger than a Russian wolfhound and twice as ugly, but very friendly. We seemed to be a hit with all of the dogs in Ireland.

Mary Butler came running when she heard the dog. She was a sweet little thing. She apologized for the dog and for the renovations going on in the house. She assured us that we would be comfortable and not have to listen to any banging while we were there. Then, she asked if she could get us some tea and cakes. Of course, we accepted. We enjoyed our little snack and the conversation with Mary. We asked her if she could serve us a light supper later. We were pretty far from anything. We hadn't seen anything in the vicinity that even looked like a place to eat. She told us she would be glad to and asked what we would like. We told her just a salad or a sandwich would be fine with tea. She told us that after supper her children would entertain us if we liked. We told her we would enjoy that very much.

Theresa asked her if she knew Bishop Forestell. She told us she knew him very well, and when Theresa told her that he was her husband's cousin, she offered to call him for Theresa to see if we could get to meet with him. As it turns out, he was out of town, so we didn't get to see him. Mary told us that he had confirmed all of her children, and she thought he was wonderful. We talked a little while longer, then went off to our room for a nap.

Around 7:00 p.m., we had a light supper. Mary had found a picture of the bishop with one of her children for Theresa. Theresa almost went into shock when she saw the picture. It was uncanny. He looked exactly like her late husband. She gave the picture to Theresa, saying that she had quite a few of them. Theresa really treasured this photo. It was so nice of Mary to give her that.

William, 17, and Marion, 11, Mary's children played music for us after supper. It was great. Marion even did an Irish dance for me. We were just so delighted with these young people. I told them that we would leave them a little something in the morning. We talked with them and laughed with them till almost 10:00 p.m. They had school in the morning, so they needed their rest. Marion was laughing at me because when she asked me where in the States we come from, so I told her. She asked me if it was really hot there in South Louisiana. I told her that it was so hot, one week this summer, that the chickens were laying hard-boiled eggs. So the next week, Roy started feeding them ice cubes, so they wouldn't get that hot again. She roared laughing. She said she couldn't wait to tell her friends that one. We had a wonderful time laughing and joking with the young people and their mother.

We learned that the eldest Butler child was in the United States performing with an Irish group that was on tour. Mary showed us pictures of him with the band and the brochure of all the places that he would be playing. She also had another child in Dublin at the university there, studying music. One of her older daughters was a music teacher. She was very proud of all of them. Well, she should be.

We talked to her for a while longer; then we went to our room and watched a little TV, and I read for a while. We really enjoyed our evening!

Thursday, October 19, 2000

We had a great breakfast. Mary could not do enough for us. What wonderful Irish hospitality.

Theresa called Helen to see how she was. She talked to Tina, her niece, who stayed with Helen for the surgery. She told her, Helen was doing good. What a relief that was for Theresa. She had not said anything, but I could tell she was really worried about her.

We told Mary that we wanted to stay in Waterford that night and asked if she would make reservations with a B&B called Woodside House run by Ann Morrisey. She said she would be glad to and did so. She gave us directions to Waterford but not before telling us about a wonderful local crystal factory nearby called Kilkenny Crystal. She said it was run by a friend, Mr. Pat Clancy, and his son, Richard. She told us that they had been artists for Waterford and decided to start their own company. They were much cheaper and just as good. This is all we needed to hear, cheaper and nearby.

We left Callan and the Butler's (which we were sad to do) and went on our way to Kilkenny Crystal. Mary gave us very good directions; we were there in no time.

We were greeted by Pat Clancy himself. He apologized for not having too much in the showroom. He explained that most of their stuff was in the stores in town. So, he joked that he could not sell us too much. Well, everything we saw was great. Mary was right. It was cheaper. We told Clancy that Mary had sent us. "Ah, a lovely woman," said he. I love the Irish braugh. It is so lilting. While we were looking around, he sang the song "Clancy, Lowered the Boom" to us. We laughed and shopped. When he saw all we were putting on the counter, he told us, "Wait a minute, ladies, you'll leave me nothing." I told him to hush and sell his wares.

Richard saw his father was having a problem and came to assist him. Several others had come in, so he assisted them. We found so many wonderful things there; I wish I would have had more money. I must say, Roy would have been proud of me. I was buying cheaper there and was having everything shipped home. Yes, Roy would be proud I didn't spend more. Hehe! Richard helped Theresa find a box. She wanted to take everything with her on the plane. He packed it, but we told him not to pack it too good. Theresa was going to add all of the other shopping that she had done that did not fit in her suitcases.

Mr. Clancy gave us each a Gaelic bookmarker for being such good customers. They were very pretty, and we both knew that it didn't cost him that much for them. It was the thought that counted, right? He also gave us directions to Waterford. So off we went again.

We drove to Waterford and Waterford Crystal, which took about three hours. Roy will be proud for sure that we bought from the Clancy's. Theresa had promised her friend Mabel that she would buy her a plate at Waterford. So she did. Talk about expensive. Everything is gorgeous there. Yes, Roy would be turning cartwheels if he saw these prices. Wow! We did get Mabel her plate but had to buy two. They did not sell only one. It was some kind of a special. So, Theresa bought her the pair. They were beautiful. Theresa decided to have them sent. Waterford did this all the time. That way, if it gets broken, they had to make it good.

After leaving Waterford, we were on our way to the B&B, which was supposed to be right down the road. Guess what? It was. Ann Morrisey greeted us and fixed us a pot of tea and told us of the Holy Cross Pub and Restaurant for supper. She said it was good food and reasonable prices. I must say, we had been pleased so far. So after we rested a while, off we went to the Holy Cross. What a name for a pub! Sounds more like a church. It was only about a mile down the road, and we had passed it on the way to the B&B.

The food was great. I had pork roast, and yes, you guessed it, Theresa had her usual, baked salmon. Everyone there was always amazed because we always had a salad. Apparently, they don't like salad as much as we do. We very seldom had a dessert. My stomach was doing good and so was Theresa's. We didn't want to rock the boat. Of course, we were drinking a lot of water and very few soft drinks. In fact, I think we only had six between us the whole time we were in Ireland. But we sure did put away the tea.

When we left the Holy Cross, we had to cross the road to go back to the B&B. Well, I had been having a great run driving in Ireland, but I was about to get shook up. I looked both ways as usual and so did my copilot, Theresa. We did not see anything coming. All of a sudden out of nowhere comes this motorcycle barreling down on me. I hit my gas pedal and gunned it. We made it. This guy must have been an American from New York because he gave me the Bronx cheer. Dumb man. He would have been more hurt than us, in a car, than on a motorcycle. He would have hit me broadside. Like we said, "Someone was watching out for us."

We got back to the room and took a shower, just to calm down. Then I read for a while before going to sleep.

Friday, October 20, 2000

Theresa and I had a good breakfast. We talked with Ann Morrisey and were surprised to learn that Mary Butler had called the night before to make sure that we had arrived safely. What a sweet lady! I wonder if she would have taken the road looking for us had we not been here.

We asked Ann if she could make reservations for us at Killarney for that night. She had thought that we were going to Cork, but we had changed our minds and wanted an extra day in Killarney so we could do the Ring of Kerry and the Dingle Peninsula. She was only too glad to make reservations for us.

She gave us directions to Killarney and the B&B we would be staying at. We would be staying at Carrowmore House owned and run by Patrick (Wreck, as we came to know him) and Kathleen McAuliffe.

The ride to Killarney was beautiful. I know that I keep saying that, but really, there is no other way to describe this country. Every turn we made was a more pretty sight than what we had just seen. We were always stopping to take photos. We took over two hundred pictures on this trip, and we really wished that we had taken more. We should have taken photos of all of our hosts but didn't, and for this, we were truly sorry. We did take one of Wreck and Kathleen though.

When we arrived at Carrowmore House, we were greeted by a beautiful rainbow. Naturally, I took pictures. The Irish weren't as smitten by the beautiful rainbows. They said they saw them all the time. We thought it a good omen. Who are we to know?

We were greeted by Kathleen who made us a pot of tea and gave us some tea cakes. We love these Irish! She told us that they did not have TVs in the rooms yet but that she did have a TV room that we were welcome to right across the hall. She took us into the TV room. The first thing that both Theresa and I noticed was an unusual doily she had on a table in the middle of the room. It had swans crocheted in it. I mean, the swans' heads and necks actually stood up, and it was so beautiful. We had never seen anything like this before. So we had a conversation about the doily. I told her that if it was missing when we were gone, she knew that we had it and were fighting over it. She said she did not make that one. She had found it at a craft show several years ago and that it was always the topic of conversation. I had never seen anything like it. So, guess what? I whipped out the camera.

We talked about the sights to be seen in Killarney, and she said she would make reservations for us for the two tours we wanted to go on, the Ring of Kerry and the Dingle Peninsula. She said they would pick us up at the front door. This was great! Her husband, Pat, came in, and she introduced us to him. She told us, "Here is my husband, his name is Pat. He will be the one to cook breakfast for you, ladies. This is his job. He used to be a wreck when he started doing it, but he is quite good at it now. This is where he got the name Wreck from. So I told him, "Don't worry, Wreck, we aren't hard to please." This stuck, and we called him Wreck from then on. It was a laugh for us. We lay down for a while before going out to eat.

They had recommended a place right down the road at the bottom of the hill on the other side of the turnaround called the Killarney Park Hotel for supper. I had prime rib roast beef for supper with a salad, and you guessed it, Theresa had baked salmon with a salad. It was a very nice place, and we really enjoyed the meal.

Saturday, October 21, 2000

Wreck cooked us a great breakfast. Dennis, the bus driver, picked us up to go on the tour. We were doing the Dingle Peninsular; Theresa had not done this one when she was here before, so she was as anxious as I was to see this one.

Dennis took us to the tour office after picking up several others for the tour. Theresa had talked to Dennis to make sure that we got the front seats in the bus so that we would have a real good view. However, when we got on the bus, there were two gentlemen in the front seats. Theresa was very upset about this and talked to Bat, our tour guide and driver for the day. He told her he was very sorry, but he had no control over that. He had reserved the seats for us, but the men had jumped into them. Bat was upset about it too. We ended up in the backseats, and we really were satisfied with this arrangement after we got going. It afforded us more room, and we're still able to see all of the sights.

It turned out to be a great day for the tour. The sun was shining, and there was a lot of beautiful scenery. I naturally took a lot of pictures.

When we got to the town of Dingle, we did some shopping. The kids were going to kill me. I bought Irish tin whistles for the grandkids!

The tour took five and a half hours. When we got back from the tour, Bat gave Theresa the tape of Irish music that he had been playing on the tour. It was a beautiful instrumental, Theresa and I think he was trying to make up to us for not having the front seats. When we returned home, we made a copy of it for me to bring home. I have enjoyed this tape a lot. I play it often. I wish that I knew what the name of it was. There are some songs that I recognize, but there are also some beautiful ones that I do not. I wish that I could put a name with the tunes.

When we got back to the B&B, we dropped off our bags, brushed our teeth, washed our faces, and then, we left for church.

Ireland trip, Sheep on hillside

We were going to the Franciscan friary in Killarney for Mass. The church was beautiful, and you guessed it, I took pictures of the altar. On the way back to the B&B, we stopped and got sandwiches to take back to the room. We were just too tired to go out and eat. Besides, it was dark out, and we didn't like to drive at night, unless we had too. Thank God, there has not been a need to.

When we got back to the room, we made a pot of tea and ate our sandwiches. We had planned on going to bed early because we were going to the Ring of Kerry tomorrow, and we wanted to be bright eyed and bushy tailed for the trip. I hate to say it, but our time in Ireland was almost up for us. We will hate to leave. We have met so many nice people here and have really enjoyed the country so much. I read a while and then went to sleep.

Sunday, October 22, 2000

Ireland trip, Thatch House

Wreck cooked breakfast again. We were still alive; he didn't get us yet. We pointed out that he only had one more day to do the deed. We all laughed about this, especially Wreck. Hehehe! Breakfast was good, and I had been amazed at how good my stomach had been doing. As Theresa pointed out, we had been really good though. Since we had been in Ireland, I had only two 7UPs and had been drinking lots of water, along with tea.

We went on the Ring of Kerry tour and only took two digital photos. It was raining so hard, I hoped the ones I did take would come out OK. We stopped at a little town and had a salad and tea and bought sandwiches for that night. We didn't want to go back out in this weather at night. It would have been beautiful scenery if the day had been better. We must make a mental note to redo this tour when we return to Ireland.

We got back to the room about 5:00 p.m., talked, and rested till 7:00. Then we brewed tea and ate. We had to drive back to Bunratty tomorrow, and then it's back to the States on Tuesday. We will miss this beautiful country and it's people. We are proud to say that our ancestors came from here. We often wonder how they could have left a land like this. It really must have been bad back then. Now, we realize why the Irish are so proud of their heritage. We had always been proud to claim that we were Irish, but now, it has a new meaning for us. It was like our souls have been at peace since we had landed here.

About 8:00 p.m., I called Roy. It is 3:00 p.m. at home, so I knew that he would be in front of the TV watching his beloved Saints. Theresa tried to call Helen again and again and again. She finally gave up and called Mary (her other daughter). She had wanted to talk to Mary anyway. Mary filled her in on the news and told her that Helen was doing fine and was getting well.

Monday, October 23, 2000

Ireland trip, sheep

Well, Monday was Wreck's last chance to do us in. Guess what? I really think that he likes us because we were still alive. After breakfast, we got ready to leave for Bunratty. We hated to say good-bye to Kathleen and Wreck. We really enjoyed being with them. Knowing that we were returning to Ashgrove House made it a little easier. This had been our first stop here in Ireland; it was only fitting that it should be our last.

We made it to Shelia and Frank Ternin's in Bunratty in only three hours. I thought that was really good. We had not met the Ternin's when we were there before. They had been on vacation, and Frank's sister, Shevaun, had been there.

We were disappointed when we saw the room. It was not the same one as before. It seems they were all filled up, so we had a smaller room with twin beds, and the bathroom was across the hall. Frank offered to get us another room at a B&B right up the road because he wanted us to be satisfied. We decided that it was only for one night, and we were close to the airport, so we would stay. I guess, we had been spoiled by Shevaun and all the others that followed her.

Frank told us about a Keileg at the castle at 7:00 p.m. They served a meal with it (salad, drinks, Irish stew, apple tart with cream, water, tea, brown bread, beets, and potato salad). So we decide to go to it. It was only two miles down the road, and it would be a great way to end our visit here. We had a pot of tea and rested awhile before going to the castle.

The Keileg was wonderful. We took a whole roll of film. The dancers were great, the girl singer was great, the emcee was very funny. We had a very enjoyable night. The guy across from us, Sid from Denver, Colorado, and several members of the audience were put on stage and danced with the group. Everyone got a big kick out of this.

That night, when we returned to the room, we were glad that we had gone. What a wonderful way to end a wonderful vacation. We both slept well.

Tuesday, October 24, 2000

We had a good breakfast and talked with several ladies at the table. We decided to call Mary Butler and tell her good-bye before we left for the airport. She had been such a treasure, and she was so concerned for us by checking on us we felt a bond with her. She was surprised to hear from us but very delighted. We told her how much we enjoyed Mr. Clancy at the Kilkenny Crystal Works. And of our purchases there. She told us that Marion had told her classmates and teachers about my chickens that lay hard-boiled eggs and what a laugh they got out of it. We were glad that we had called her. We wish we had taken photos of her and the children. As we said before, hindsight is a wonderful thing.

We met the people who would be taking our room. I don't know how he is going to sleep in that twin bed. He must be 6' 3" and the beds were short. She is tall too. Anyway, Shelia told us to please stay awhile because our plane did not leave until later in the afternoon. So we did stay for a while, but we were anxious to find our way back to the airport.

We drove to the airport, and I dropped off Theresa and the luggage, then went to return the car. I was glad to return the car in one piece, especially with the side mirrors still intact. Theresa swore that I hit them on other side mirrors, but they were still on the car. Hehehe!

I rode the little bus back to the airport and met Theresa. I got a wheelchair for her, and I schlep it. We checked in the luggage and got our boarding passes, and then we went to the duty-free shop. There we spent more money.

Theresa had told me about this duty-free shop and how wonderful the stuff was. She had underestimated it. I found wonderful things. I used up all the rest of my Irish pound except for eighteen. I had wanted to take some of the money home with me to show the grandchildren. They will get a kick out of it. I bought water balls with leprechauns in or on them, little leather coin purses in green with a soft material inside that would be great for rosary beads, things for golfers (my brothers), things for the drinkers (my brothers), and the greatest paperweight, which I will keep. I really had a marvelous time in this store. (It's a woman thing.) I was proud of my purchases!

We left the duty-free shop and went to a small food court to eat a little lunch while waiting for our flight. We had worked up an appetite shopping. We got sandwiches and water and ate. We turned in our sales tax form so that they would return it to us. We went to a smoking area because that little vice of mine was crying for a cigarette. We stayed there until our flight was called. We filled out our exit visas while we were waiting there. We were on a roll.

Aer Lingus had a baggage handlers' strike while we were in Ireland, and it had shut down one day. We were hoping that they would do it again so that we could stay a day or two longer at the airlines' expense, but it did not happen. Oh well!

We had a great flight home. We each had two seats to ourselves. They had assigned us an exit row seat so they had to move us. This worked out in our favor because we ended up with more room. Theresa slept and ate. I read and ate on the flight.
When we arrived in Boston, they had two wheelchairs waiting for us, but only one skycap. He wheeled us through customs and the airport, got our luggage, and took very good care of us. He was amazing.

Richard met us with the limo. We had a great ride back to Theresa's. Richard asked about our trip, and we had him laughing all the way home. We stopped and picked up Subway and Dunkin' Donuts for dinner and breakfast in the morning.

When we got to Theresa's, we bid Richard good-bye and thanked him for a smooth ride and for being so nice. He had really been very good to us, so we tipped him a little extra. He was pleased.

I called Roy when we got to Theresa's. He sounded happy to hear from me. I know that he is glad that I was back in the States. He is always afraid that I will get sick like I did that time when I was on a cruise. I came down with pneumonia, and he could not get to me. He thought that he should help me when things like that happen. He was right, of course, but at the time, he could not, so there is no sense for him to beat himself up about it.

We were both very tired; it had been a long day, so we ate our sandwiches and drank some tea and went to bed after talking awhile. Seems as though we always had so much to say to each other; we laughed a lot together. What a jewel I had found that first day in that chat room.

Wednesday, October 25, 2000

Well, I was up earlier than I thought. I had coffee and two Dunkin' donuts, mmmm good. We can't get Dunkin' Donuts in Houma, Louisiana. So, this is a real treat for me. I was trying not to smoke too much for Theresa's sake. I have done real well, hope that it continues. Roy would really like that. Theresa and I have taken it really easy today. I took my shower around 2:00 p.m. I wanted to wash my hair today, so it would be decent for my trip home tomorrow.

Pat and Helen came over at 4:00 p.m. We read our journals to them. They roared laughing and so did we. Sometimes, it was hard for us to read; we laughed so hard. They really thought that I was nuts. They were a little upset with us because we didn't bring them each an Irishman. We explained we did not have room in our luggage. Besides, we would have brought back one for Theresa if we had the room.

Helen left at 6:30 p.m., so Pat and Theresa went after a salad and sandwiches for us. I stayed at the apartment. I had only one clean outfit left for tomorrow and had my caftan on, so I stayed.

They returned with food, and we ate and laughed a lot more. Pat said she could just picture Mr. Healy going up those regal gentle steps, and Theresa's bag going off and the restaurant manager's face when I pushed him in the car with Theresa. He didn't know what was happening. (Poor stud muffin.) I could see it in his face; he didn't know what we would do to him. Crazy old American women. We could have knocked him in the head with our canes and threw him in the back and ravaged him. We really messed up there and missed our chance to show him what life is really about.

Pat stayed till 9:30 p.m. Theresa got on the net, and I lay down after taking my medicine. Going home tomorrow.

Thursday, October 26, 2000

I had a good night. When I got up, I made coffee and had the last two donuts. They were good. I would miss Dunkin' Donuts, but too much of a good thing can be bad for you.

Theresa and I reminisced and then ate lunch. I got dressed and finished packing when something hit me to check my ticket. Good thing, the plane left at 3:16 p.m. Oh my god, it was 2:20 p.m.!

Theresa and I flew out the door with the luggage to get to the airport. We were at the car struggling with the luggage when Bob happened along and came to our rescue. He was out walking the dogs. One of the dogs jumped in the car and had decided that he was going with us. When Bob tried to get him out, he snapped at him and jumped on me. Oh no, we don't need this right now. Theresa called the dog, and he jumped out of the car, thinking she was going somewhere else, and he was going with her. She jumped in the car, and we were on our way.

Theresa had told me that it took forty-five minutes to an hour to get to the airport. I was praying all the way. She took the back way, and we made it for 3:00 p.m. I could not believe this; neither could she. I had just enough time to check in and get to the gate. I couldn't believe this.

Theresa and I really didn't have time for our good-byes, and I guess that it was better that way. We would have gotten all dewy-eyed and flustered with the hugging, so I guess this really was the best.

We can never explain to anyone just what we felt about this trip. It was like "Going Home" with a "Dear Friend." A friend that will be in our hearts for the rest of our lives and after. How we ever got through three weeks together without even a cross word between us is beyond both of us. But miracle of miracles, that is just what we did. The people we met along the way were very gracious and kind. They were good ambassadors for their country. They will always have a warm spot in our hearts. We both hope that someday, we can return there and do it again. But then, you know you can never recreate the past.

New Orleans Journal

Wednesday, June 6, 2001

Theresa and Helen will be arriving today from Portland, Maine. Helen is Theresa's daughter. The reason they are coming here is because Theresa's brother, Dick, and his wife, Marvis, are celebrating their fiftieth wedding anniversary Friday. They are having a big party at the Treasure Chest. You know, with food and all. Another reason is because they miss me. Dick and Marvis graciously had invited Roy and I to go to the celebration. I will, but Roy will not be able. Theresa and Helen will be staying with us because Dick's children will be staying there with them, and I miss them more. Their sister, Helen, and her family will be staying at a motel not far from their home. They are driving in from Maine. There are some family members from Florida arriving for the bash also. It should be something.

Well, as usual, the weather is bad. Whenever Theresa comes in, there is sure to be plenty of rain. Roy says this is great because right now, we can use it. The drive to New Orleans airport wasn't too bad. I was concerned for Helen though. This is her first flight, and she has a fear of bad weather. She suffers so, wish there were something they could do to help her and people like her. Roy had an aunt that was terrified of bad weather, but that is another story.

When we got to the airport, we were running a little behind time. Roy always leaves with plenty of time to spare, but the weather held us up. Dick was waiting for us when we got to the gate. He said that the airlines had just posted a delay on their flight. It would be an hour late because of weather. So we ended up with plenty of time. The weather was really bad, lots of thunder and lightning, along with the rain. I was hoping that they didn't have to tie Helen down on the plane. Hehehe!

After about an hour, we found out the plane was circling the airport but, because of the weather, could not land. Lord, Helen will be a mess. The three of us talked. I was telling Dick that my daughter, Mia, and I had made arrangements for Theresa, Helen, Mia, and her son, Jordan, and I to stay downtown at the Quarter House in the French Quarter on Friday for a week. We thought that they would enjoy that, and we had a week on our time-share that we had to use by December, so we did that. We would keep it for a week. My brother, Rudy, and his family were arriving on Tuesday for a convention here, and that way, we could visit with them too without having the hour drive. It was a two-bed room, two-bath suite with a small kitchen, so we thought that this would be something different for them, and they would be close to where all the action was. It also had a nice living room with a pullout bed in the couch. So we knew that we had plenty of room. One bedroom had a king-size bed, and the other was a queen size. I was really hoping that we could talk Theresa and Helen into staying an extra day or two. They would be leaving on Tuesday, and Rudy and the family would be arriving on Tuesday, and I really wanted them to meet. I had talked about Theresa so much to them that they felt like they already knew her.

Finally, one and a half hours late, the plane is pulling up to the Jetway. Naturally, they are never the first one off. They are going to have to wait for a wheelchair for Theresa. There they are. Oh my, Helen is as white as a sheet and shaking. Her eyes are like big saucers. She looks like she just was scared out of her wits. Theresa looks great, as usual.

We greet each other, and Helen says, "I can't believe it, we are back on the ground." We all laughed, knowing that we may have trouble getting her back here in a week to go home.

We all visited for a while, and then Dick left to go to his house, and we were on our way to Houma. The weather had eased up a bit, so Helen had calmed down a good bit.

Theresa said when they were on their way into New Orleans and the weather got bad, Helen was very afraid. Theresa told her to close her eyes and start praying because that is what she was planning on doing. She said every time they hit an air bump or got a flash of lightning, Helen would say, "Shit, shit, shit." She said that Helen was not the only one saying this; she could hear several others doing the same thing, some of them using worse language than that. She said Helen shook the whole time.

When we got home, they rested awhile, and then we ate. I had fixed a chicken okra gumbo and a jambalaya, along with some fresh sliced tomatoes, cucumbers, and Cajun potato salad. They loved all of it. We laughed because I told them that they would be spoiled by the time they left for the fresh vegetables from Roy's garden. Fresh eggs too. This was the first time that Theresa had been to my home, and I was hoping to make a good impression.

Debra, Kristen, and Eric came over after supper to visit. Eric loves to tease Theresa. It was still raining and thundering out. All of a sudden, this big clap of thunder and lightning sounded, and we all thought that Helen was going to jump into Eric's lap. Eric didn't know what was happening. I wish you could have seen the looks on both of their faces when it happened. It was priceless.

We talked a lot, and we got on the computer to let all of our chat-room buddies know that they had arrived safely. We did not stay on long because we were all getting tired. I had not made any plans for us for tomorrow. I thought that we could have a day of rest, or if they wanted, we would go somewhere.

Thursday, June 7, 2001

Well, we finally made it up. I had planned a treat for Helen for lunch. I was going to fry some shrimp and french fries for her, along with tomatoes, lettuce, and cucumbers. She loves shrimp. She was so pleased, you could see the look of delight on her face as she sunk her teeth into it.

Oh, I have to put this in here, or Theresa will kill me. They claim that I am a wonderful cook. She and Helen never ate Cajun food before, and they are sure that they put on a few pounds, that they had tried so hard to get rid of before coming on this trip.

After lunch, we walked in the yard, swung on the swing, looked at the chickens, and just yacked. We did a lot of that. They couldn't get over all the chickens that Roy had and all the vegetables that Roy had growing in the garden. Roy took them down to the arena to show that to them also.

I showed them pictures of the Quarter House, and they were impressed. Hell, I was impressed also. We planned on what we would take with us tomorrow. I had gotten a few boxes so we could pack some things to take with us, like coffee, tea, sugar, cereal, bread, milk, eggs, tomatoes, cucumbers, onions, potatoes, in other words, a survival kit. We were going to be well prepared.

We kind of goofed off most of the day, and for supper, we had leftovers from last night. Theresa called her brother, Dick, and told him that we would check into the Quarter House around 4:00 p.m., and then we would get settled and go to the Treasure Chest for the party at 7:00 p.m. He wanted to come downtown to get us, but we vetoed that idea; we could always get a limo or a cab if I don't feel like driving at night (which is one of my quirks, I hate driving at night.) He would have enough to deal with. He still had people coming in for the party and was meeting all of them and getting them settled at the motel he had made arrangements with. He got them a special deal through the Treasure Chest. Good thinking, Dick. See, I am not the only one who looks for special prices. They always tease me because I am always going on Priceline.com and getting cheap fares for airlines when I go somewhere, and motels too.

Oh, I must mention that we had showers off and on all day. This is in keeping with Theresa's reputation for keeping it cool and moist here for her stay. After all, June is usually a hot month here. Fat chance with Theresa here!

Friday, June 8, 2001

We are up and moving, that is a good sign. We have a light breakfast and start packing to go to New Orleans. We decide that we will stop at the supermarket here and get bread and milk and the perishable things that we want to bring so we don't have to deal with it when we get there. I have a large ice chest, so there is no danger of it spoiling. We also decide to get some lunch meats and other meats. We are into saving money. Around 2:00 p.m., we leave the house and make our stops on the way. Oh, did I mention that it was raining again. Oh yes, Theresa's reputation is still intact.

When we arrive in New Orleans, it is pouring. The Quarter House is on Chartes Street. The parking facility is a block and a half away, so we decide that we are going to check in and unload; then I will go park the car. There is only one problem. We can't get out of the car. It is raining so hard. All the porters are huddled under the awning, and I don't blame them. They have an umbrella, but then so do I (in the trunk of the car). It doesn't take a brain surgeon to figure out that we are going to be soaked by the time we finish unloading, but we can't just sit there. So I brave it. Open the trunk and get the porter to start unloading. I give Theresa the umbrella and Helen the parka to put on so they don't get soaked. I was a lost cause. I looked like a drowned rat. Anyway, we get unloaded and to the desk, and lucky us, they say that our suite is not ready yet and will be another half hour to forty-five minutes. So, I leave Theresa with the luggage and groceries in the lobby, and Helen and I take the car and go to the parking garage. Then, we get to wade through the water to get back.

When we return, Theresa is still waiting in the lobby, and naturally, there is no smoking in the lobby, so I decide to have a cigarette outside in the rain, with the umbrella, of course.

Well, we finally get to the suite and talk about luxury. Wow! We decide that I will take the room with the king-size bed in it for Mia, Jordan, and I. The reason for that was because the bed was so high off the floor that Theresa could not hike it up there that far. Usually when they have a bed this high off the floor, they have a stool for you to step on. We looked all over for one but could not find one. Hehehe! We are happy that each of the bathrooms has a hot tub. It even has a safe in one of the closets for us. We are impressed. Everything was there for us. Mia and Jordan would be joining us in the morning. She had to work tonight.

We decide to unpack our waterlogged luggage and groceries. Theresa's luggage was so soaked that we had to dry out her passport. We went through the rest of the stuff and discovered that the passport was the worst of it. Our clothes are dry. We take our showers and get ready to go to the Treasure Chest for the party.

The desk called us at 6:45 p.m. to tell us that our taxi was waiting for us. We had decided to take a cab; with all the rain and etc., we thought it would be best. So off we go.

We arrive at the Treasure Chest and go to the banquet room, where the celebration is being held. It was really set up nice, with tables and then three buffet tables with people to help you with your choices and to take them to the table for you. Wow, Dick and Marvis really went all out for this. It is nice. The food was presented wonderfully and tasted just as great. Dick and Marvis were beaming as they greeted their guest. It is so nice to see a happily married couple. You don't get to experience many fiftieth wedding anniversary parties.

We sat with Theresa's sister Helen S. and her family (her daughter Tina, husband, Jerry, daughter Caitlyn, and niece Mildred). They had driven in from Maine, and we talked about their experiences on the road. Oh, I must say that Tina and Jerry's twelve-year-old daughter is disabled. She is in a wheelchair, but she is a very happy and bright child.

After the meal, they gave out all the speeches and did we laugh at what their boys said. They talked about their lives growing up with Marvis and Dick. They thanked all for coming, especially the ones who had traveled from Maine, Florida, and California. Then, they had a surprise for all of us. Dick's barbershop quartet was there, and they entertained us with some of their songs. It was such a treat to hear them sing again. Everyone enjoyed it so. After that, everyone visited with each other. Soon some of us decide to go try our luck at the slots and tables. Heck, why not? We were there weren't we!

Well, as usual most of us contributed to the economy of the city of Kenner. A few of us came out with a few dollars ahead. I was one of the lucky ones! Love that Treasure Chest. Roy and I go there about once a month and try our luck.

When we got back to the banquet room, we were going to take a cab back to the city, but Dick and Marvis insisted on driving us back. Dick said that way he would know how to find us again. We gave everyone the phone number so they could get in touch with us on Saturday.

Saturday, June 9, 2001

Mia will be here today. (She lives in Slidell, about thirty miles away.) She and her friend Lynette were planning on taking Helen, Tina, Jerry, and Mildred for a night in the French Quarter. Burbon Street was only two blocks away, so they could walk. Theresa and I had decided to babysit Jordan, along with Helen S. and Caitlyn.

When Mia and Jordan arrived around 8:30 a.m., she brought beignets from Café du Mond with her. What a treat for us; Helen had never had them and had heard of them. So we all sat around, enjoyed our coffee and beignets, and yacked; it was old home week. Jordan loves his Teesa (that is what he calls Theresa), and he falls in love with Helen also. He hugs his Teesa and is just happy to be with her again. She has sure made a conquest there. We were going to take a swim, but guess what, it was raining. Hehehe!

We fix some food for us to eat and prepare fruit for us to have to snack on. I made a potato salad and cut up tomatoes and cucumbers and boiled some eggs so that we would not have too much to do later. This worked well for us. We could always go find something to eat and saved us much. We would not need to eat out hardly at all.

About 6:30 p.m., the desk calls to say that we have guest in the lobby. I forgot to say that this is a very secure place in the Quarter. Helen went down to bring them up. They are more impressed with our suite than we were. Theresa and I were disappointed because Helen S.

and Caitlyn decided to stay at the motel. We thought that we would have time to visit with them. They told us of all their travels in the city during the day. They were doing the sightseeing thing. Theresa and I had already done that in our younger days. Don't think we could handle all of the walking again. Oh yes, and we took pictures.

We waited for Lynette to arrive. (Lynette is always late, so we always tell her that we are leaving one hour before we plan to so that she will be here on time. This works for us.) After Lynette arrived and visited for a while, they left for their night in the Quarter.

Theresa, Jordan, and I decided to chill out. Jordan is a delightful but very devilish child. He is a typical boy. He played with his toys that Mia had brought for him and watched the Discovery Channel. (He loves the Discovery Channel.) When we decided to go to bed, Jordan decided that he was going to sleep with Teesa. That was OK with us, didn't last long though; he ended up with me.

We were shocked when the partiers arrived back at the suite. We had expected them to stay out much longer. They were tired from the trip and all the festivities, and they had taken Caitlyn to the Audubon Zoo that day, so they decided to make it an early night. What a shame, they couldn't have enjoyed it more. We had offered them a place to sleep, but they decided that they should go back to their motel.

Of course, Lynette was not with them. She, as usual, had run into some friends and decided to make a night of it. This is typical Lynette.

Sunday, June 10, 2002

When we got up, still no Lynette. Oh, well, she will show up, and sure enough, halfway through lunch, she did. Jordan was excited; he had his Teesa and Helen to play with.

We decided that we would go to Harrah's casino later today to try our luck. Mia's husband, Steve, was in town, so he would come take care of Jordan while we were gone. He works for an oil company, and he had to be back in the morning. It made it nice though for us; we didn't have to take Jordan out to Kenner for his nanny to care for him.

So we just lay around all day, and then around 6:00 p.m., we got ready to go to the casino. It was not but a few blocks away, so we decided that we didn't want to walk and we didn't want to go get the car, so we took a cab.

This was my first visit to Harrah's. After all the hype that they had given it, we were disappointed. Thought that it would be much bigger. I understand now that they have opened the second floor, so it is. We donated to the cause (New Orleans economy) but didn't seem to have any luck. Finally, I was about $100 down, so I decided that it was time for me to quit. I found Theresa and Helen, but Helen had just hit it big. She was winning and didn't want to leave. So Mia and I decided to leave them there and relieve Steve. That way, they would get to see each other for a while before he had to go back.

As luck would have it, when we got to the suite, just as he was trying to call us, his shop had called and needed him back there. So Mia and I decided to watch TV for a while; Jordan was not ready to call it a day yet. Where does all of his energy come from?

About midnight, Theresa and Helen arrived all excited. Helen had won enough money to pay for her trip. She was thrilled. Theresa had lost, but not really much. So they had a great night. We decided to have a bedtime snack; they wanted popcorn, and as luck would have it, we had brought some microwave popcorn with us. They scorched the first batch, what a smell. Not being deterred, they popped another batch. After that, we all decided to go to bed.

I was sleeping so sound when all of a sudden, I could hear something ringing. I reached for the phone and looked at the time. It was 3:00 a.m. No one was on the phone. Then, I realized it was the smoke alarm. I got up and went into the kitchen, living room section, and did not see any smoke. I woke Mia up; that wasn't hard. She was half awake from the noise. She got up, and then Helen showed up, and the phone started ringing. It was the desk. They wanted to know if we had a fire because the alarm at the desk had gone off. We told them that we did not see any smoke. Mia went outside in the hallway to see if there was a fire there. No smoke! Of course, I could still smell the burnt popcorn, but no smoke. Well, now what? I want to tell you that alarm was going crazy. Helen was trying to wake up Theresa. She had taken a sleeping pill, and we could not wake her. She just rolled over and told Helen to come back to bed. It was too early to get up. So, I went in their room and tried to get her up. Well, she finally got up!

The desk called again and told us that the alarm was still ringing. Gee! They must be brain surgeons down there, we could hear it. We told them that it was still ringing here too, and they needed to send someone up to stop it. In the meantime, we had discovered that there was a leak in the living room ceiling, and it was pouring through the smoke alarm. (Oh, did I forget to mention, that we were having one of our famous thunder, lightning, and very heavy rain? Well, we were.) Mia was running around trying to figure out how to shut off the alarm. (Jordan was still sleeping, and we were praying that he did not wake up.) Helen had gotten the wastebasket from the kitchen and had it under the leak. What a mess.

I guess you have realized by now that at 3:00 a.m. on a Monday morning, there are no maintenance people around. So they sent up the desk clerk. Naturally, the first thing that she smells is the burnt popcorn and my cigarette. (You know that I had to have a cigarette.) She had talked to the engineer, and he had told her what to do to shut the thing off.

She was going to try to take the front off of the smoke detector and try to shut it off. Well, this child was about 4' 9" tall. She could not reach the dumb thing. It was a very high ceiling. So she got a broom and tried that. After she realized this would not work, she got a chair to climb on. She was climbing on the chair when I realized that this child (she looked like a child, turns out she was twenty-eight) was pregnant (found out later, she was eight months). Oh my god. We made her get down. Mia told her, "Tell me what to do and I will do it." So she jumps up on the chair, and I realized that the water is still pouring through this thing, and it is still going off, so it still has electricity to it. I told her to get down before she electrocuted herself and told the clerk to call someone else. So she calls the house engineer at his home. She tells him that we can't shut the thing off because of the water pouring through the detector, and we were afraid of her being electrocuted. He said he didn't realize that. (Like I said, they were brain surgeons.) In the meantime, Mia is looking at the breaker box, so she gets on the phone with him, and they decide what she needs to do. Hurrah! She finds the right breaker to turn off, and the alarm goes off. By this time, we had listened to this thing for forty-five minutes. Our ears would be ringing for some time to come. What a relief. We could not believe that Jordan and Theresa had slept through all of this. Oh yes, Theresa had gone back to bed when she realized there was no danger. Those pills really knocked her out.

The clerk tells us that they would transfer us to another unit now. Well, we were not about to start packing up at 3:45 in the morning and moving to a different suite. We did not feel that we were in any danger, so we told her that we would prefer to stay there. Thank God for the wastebasket. She then said that someone would be up to fix the thing in the morning and clean up the mess. We told her to please not make it too early because we needed some sleep after this. By this time, we are awake, so we talked till around 6:00 a.m., then went back to bed. What a night!

Around 9:00 a.m., yes, 9:00 a.m., the men show up to fix the mess. There is a leak in the roof, so they have to fix that, plus change the smoke detector. Guess what happened to our sleep, with them walking on the roof above us? Right, we didn't get any. By 1:00 p.m., we were dragging, and we had still not heard from the manager, so Mia called for her. She was busy on another line, and they wanted to know if there was a problem. *Was there a problem?* Mia gives them a thumbnail sketch of our night and that the electrician still had not made it there to fix the smoke detector. They said that they knew about it, and they were going to have the manager call back and would send the electrician right up. Next thing we knew, there was a knock on the door. It was the electrician. He came in, and then he changed the smoke detector and tested it. We really needed to hear this thing again.

By 5:30 p.m., we still had not heard from the manager. Mia was fuming, and believe me, I was not too happy either, so she called for her again; she was gone for the day. Now Mia was mad. She told us that we were not calling for her again, and if she did not hear from her by 11:00 a.m. tomorrow when we had to go meet with the people running the condo that they would get an earful. *It is not a good thing to get Mia angry!* They were going to try to sell us another one, and Mia and Steve were considering getting one for them.

Theresa had talked to Dick earlier, and he wanted us to go to supper with him and Marvis that night. Mia had to work, and she was taking Jordan to his nanny's to spend the night. So we got ready to go out with Dick.

When Dick and Marvis arrived, the front desk called us. Helen went down and brought them up. Theresa wanted them to see this place. They were impressed as were the rest of us. We decided that we would go to the Treasure Chest for supper, and then we could gamble a little after. Off we go.

We had a great meal and visited. Then we hit the slots. I must say that Dick does not gamble, but he is a great watchdog for all of us. He goes around checking on us. When he found me the third time, he liked to have went into shock. I had been playing the dollar machine, and I had hit. I had hit! I had won about $400, so he offered to go cash it in for me. I gave him all of the cups that were full. I had one that was only about one-third full, so I decided to continue playing with that. (I should have quit.) So I feed back the money in this cup. Got to keep the economy rolling. Dick told me that Marvis had won about $100 also. Marvis only plays the nickel machines, so just think what she would have done had she been playing the $1 one. So we were doing great; now was the perfect time to leave. So we did. Helen and Theresa had not fared as well, but they were happy. They would be leaving to go home tomorrow, so they wanted to get some rest.

Dick told Theresa and Helen that he would pick them up to take them to the airport the next day. She told him that we had checked to see what the shuttle would cost, and they had decided to take the shuttle. Well, I guess you know that he would have none of that. He was coming to take them, and that was that. So that was that! Dick drove us back to the Quarter House. When we got there, an ambulance was blocking the drive. It was Mia and her partner. She had decided she wanted to show her partner how the other half lives, so she was giving him the tour. (She scared everyone in the place when she got there; they were in uniform and with the ambulance, and they thought something had happened to one of the guest.) Never a dull moment! (I think it is the heat here that does this to us.) We parted with Dick and Marvis and told him we would see them tomorrow afternoon.

Mia and Elvis (her partner) decided they would eat before leaving. So they raided the frig, ate, and then left.

We had had enough excitement and decided to go to bed and get some rest.

Monday, June 11, 2002

Well, by the time we had to go to our meeting with the condo people, Mia was in rare form. We still had not heard from the manager. Mia was keeping her cool though. She said she would not take it out on them, but they would hear about it. We decided that we were taking Jordan with us because Theresa and Helen were packing to leave that afternoon, and we did not want them to have to run after him. Plus, we knew that he would raise three kinds of hell if his momma left him again.

We arrived at our meeting. Naturally, they are not ready for us. What is with these people? Why is it when you make appointments with people, they like to keep you waiting? I am including all professional people too. Like doctors. I think that they should have to deduct from their bill when they do this. They are wasting my time and charging me too. I have voiced this opinion to numerous doctors, and for some reason now, I don't have to wait as long as I used too.

When the fellow that is giving us the tour greets us, he makes the mistake of asking, "How are you enjoying your stay here at the Quarter House?" Well, this is all that it takes for Mia to tell him. Poor thing, he was between a rock and a hard place. He got right on the phone and called the manager, and we were to meet with her as soon as we finished with this kind man.

We took the tour, and we were very impressed. Mia and Steve were considering buying a time-share for themselves, so she told him that she would think about it. It all depended on what the manager said to us. He gave us each a really nice canvas carryall. This is good. We can give them to Theresa and Helen to remember their stay here. We left there to go meet with the manager.

When we got there, Mia told me, "Now, Momma, let me do the talking, I will take care of everything." She said she didn't want me getting upset. I told her that this was my intention to begin with. Soon the manager came. She told us that she was sorry that we had experienced a little trouble. A LITTLE TROUBLE! WHERE DID THEY GET ALL OF THESE BRAIN SURGEONS?

Mia talked for about ten minutes about the alarm going off for forty-five minutes and the fact that it was 3:00 a.m. and that we couldn't get back to sleep and we could not do what we had planned to do the next day with our out-of-town guest because we were too tired. Then at 9:00 a.m., the maintenance people were there, and the roofers had to *bang, bang* to fix the roof above us. The electrician did not get there till 2:00 p.m. to fix the smoke detector. Believe me she got an earful. The manager asked Mia, "What would it take to make you happy?" Mia told her, "Offer me something because believe me the association is going to hear about all of this." So she offered us a comp of a three-day stay at a date of our choosing. The only thing she asked is that we let her know a few days ahead of time so she could make the arrangements. Mia told her, "That will work, put it in writing." So she did.

When we were waiting for the elevator to go back to the suite, I was looking at the movies they had for rent. I told Mia, "I would like to see *The Perfect Storm*, so let's find out how much it costs." The manager heard me, and says, "Oh, here take it, and bring it back when you are finished with it." So we got a three-day comp and a free movie. I was pleased.

When we got back to the suite, we gave Theresa and Helen the carryalls and told them what had happened and showed them the movie. They were impressed. Leave it to Mia! She even impresses her momma! I have always wondered where I got this child from. After that, we sat down and watched the movie. It was a great movie. Wish it could have ended better, but then it was a true story.

Not long after that, Dick arrived to take the travelers to the airport. I had done my bit and tried to talk them into staying till Friday but was unable to accomplish this. Theresa would have, but Helen had to get back to work the next day. So we had to part. I went down with them to the lobby. I didn't want to go to the airport 'cause I am a big baby when it comes to seeing loved ones leave. They promised to call when they got home and let me know that all was well. We hugged, and they were gone.

Mia and I had the condo till Friday. My brother and his family were arriving the next day. So we could stay there for a few more days and be with them. This turned out perfect. Could not have done better if I had planned it.

Bye all, till the next trip!

Oklahoma Trip

Well, here we are again, planning another trip. It was August; Theresa and I wanted to go somewhere again. So, we put our heads together and decided that Oklahoma would be next.

We have a friend in the chat room that is always saying that no one ever comes to visit her. They always tell her that they are coming but never do. She is in a wheelchair and has been having a lot of trouble with her eyes; we decided that we would go visit her while she could see our beautiful selves in all our glory.

Theresa's brother, Dick, had been having trouble with cellulites in his legs. He had been in and out of the hospital the last few months with it, so we decided that she would fly here. That way, she could see her brother, and then we could drive to Oklahoma to visit Gert for a few days. Good plan, huh?

I made all of the arrangements online for Theresa to take a flight from Portland to New Orleans. She trusts me so. The fact that she is afraid to do anything like that for fear of messing it up has nothing to do with it. We are excited.

September 11, 2001

You will not believe what has taken place today. Some al Qaeda terrorists hijacked four planes and crashed them into the World Trade Center in New York (one in the north tower and another in the south tower), one in the Pentagon building in Washington, DC, and the other crashed in a field in Pennsylvania. Authorities believed that the fourth one was headed for the White House. The passengers on this plane rushed the hijackers, and in the struggle, the plane went down. During all of this, it was all over the news, and they showed it live.

They were taping near there, and the cameraman was distracted by the plane directly overhead, so he jerked his camera up and got it just as it was going into the first tower. After that, we saw everything live. It was horrible. What a waste of human life. We watched in awe as firefighters, policemen, emergency medical people, and anyone who could save the people they could. All a lot of us could do was sit in disbelief, cry, and pray. Most of America was glued to the TV screen. I pray that I never see anything like this again. I pray for the children of the world who are going to inherit this mess. Why does the human race do this to each other? That is the age-old question.

When we got in the chat room that night, everyone was talking about it. Let's face it; it was the topic of conversation all over the world. Some of the ladies were asking Theresa and I if we would fly again. I told them that I am a fatalist and that I would because God is not going to take me a minute before my time no matter where I am. Theresa was very hesitant about her answer, and I sensed some fear in her. She told everyone that she was not sure if she would or not.

She and I discussed it later, and she was sure that she would not fly again. I asked her to wait for a while and see what happens. It was still another month before she was scheduled to fly here, and I felt that the confidence of the American people would be restored by then. She agreed to do that, so I felt better.

Gert, our friend that we were going to visit, was concerned that we would not come because of the terrorist attack. I told her to let it sit awhile, that after the initial shock, Theresa would probably let her logic take over. Right now, we were all too emotional about it. So that is what we all did.

Theresa and I talked many times about this in the weeks to come. She decided about a week before she was to come that she would fly again. I was thrilled. I just could not see those assholes getting away with the fear they had induced on the American people.

Six days before Theresa arrived, her brother, Dick, was operated on for a subdorial hematoma (blood around the brain). She was very concerned about him. We decided when she arrived on Saturday that we would go with her to see how he was doing. She was very glad about this. She had been talking to Marvis (her sister-in-law) every day about his condition, and it was not good at first, but he was improving. She was very glad that she was scheduled to be here now. Isn't it strange how the Lord works in mysterious ways?

Saturday, October 14, 2001

"Well, it is raining again. Theresa must be arriving today," was the way Roy greeted me when I got up. I laughed and replied, "Yep, she is arriving today." Later, we drove to the airport in the rain to pick up Theresa and go to see Dick.

Theresa said her trip from Maine to New Orleans was very smooth. She had a good flight. Then, she teased Roy about the rain. We went and picked up her luggage, and Roy went to get the car.

Dick had been released from the hospital and was at his home. So we were on our way there. Good thing I had gotten the directions from Marvis to get to the house because Theresa said she didn't know how. As many times as she has been here, she never drove when she was here, so she didn't remember.

After making a few wrong turns, we finally arrived at the house. Dick was downstairs in the family room. They had set up a hospital bed for him there. So we were able to sit and chat and visit with him. He looked great for all he had been through. He had four extra holes in his head now where they had drilled to relieve the pressure on his brain. We didn't stay too long; we were afraid that it would tire Dick too much, and we knew that Theresa was tired out from her trip. It was good that we went though because Theresa could see for herself that he was doing great. It took a big worry off her mind. Even though they live far apart, Dick and Theresa are very close. So off we go in the rain on our way to Houma.

When we arrived at home, we were all hungry, so I fixed us all a snack. Of course, we did a lot of talking too. It had been four months since we had been able to talk face-to-face. After a while, we decided to let everyone in the chat room know that Theresa had arrived safe and had visited with her brother. We didn't stay online long; we were tired and need to get some rest. We were leaving in the morning for Oklahoma. Gert still did not believe that we were driving, and her husband, John, didn't believe it either. Were they in for a shock!

Monday, October 15, 2001

Well, here we go again; Theresa and I are off. Roy thought that we should get up early and leave for about 7:00 a.m. We vetoed that in a hurry. We left about 10:00 a.m.

We were on our way to Oklahoma City and Gertrude. We had made reservations to stay in Marshall, Texas, for the night at the Comfort Inn. That way, we would make it there tomorrow, and we would not be so worn out from driving. We always make sure that we do not go too long each day. We may be seniors, but we were going to be sensible about this.

We had no problems getting to Marshall, Texas. We checked in, and then we went to supper at a buffet restaurant just down the road. It was very nice, and we enjoyed our meal. Then, we came back to the room, and we took our showers, talked awhile, watched the news on TV, and went to bed.

Tuesday, October 16, 2001

Theresa and I got up, had coffee, and checked out of the motel. We were a little concerned about driving through Dallas. You know how it is when you have to drive through a large city and you don't know the roads. As it turns out, we went through the city without any problems. The roads were well marked. We saw signs that said Oklahoma City, so we were relieved; that meant that we had done it right. Whew!

When we got to Oklahoma City, we had a lot of little turns to make, and guess what? We missed one. Did you think that we were going to do everything right? So being the intelligent sex, we stopped at a store and called Gert.

When Gert answered the phone, I said, "Where are we? Come find us, we are lost. We missed a turn somewhere." Gert started laughing. She asked, "Don't I even get a hello?" We explained to her where we were, and she told us, "Don't move, we will be right there to get you." We did move though; we went into the store and got us some drinks and snacks to take to the motel, and then we waited outside for Gert and John.

We were not out of the store long when they arrived. John got out of the car and said to me, "Hello, Grasshopper." I was in a green pants suit, and he would call me that from that moment on. We went to the car and hugged Gert. We forgot to say that

Gert is handicapped since she had a stroke several years ago and uses a wheelchair to get around in. We were very glad to see them. They told us that we were not far from the motel that we had reservations at, and we could just follow them there. This was great. We told him to take his time and make sure that we were always behind them. We did not want to get lost again; once a day is quite enough. We made all of the turns and everything very well. We had the light, and for some reason, I looked to my left, and this car was barreling down on us. I hit the break just in time. Who said that seniors don't have good reflexes? That car missed us by two hairs. We were shook up a lot by this. The guy in the car had the nerve to shoot us a dirty look and scream something at us. We continued on and made it to the motel and checked in.

When we got to the room, the topic of conversation was our near-miss accident. John decided to go home because he was not interested in women talk, and he knew that we would talk for quite a while. So we told him to go on, and when Gert was ready to go home, we would call him. They only lived a few blocks away, and it would not take long for him to return.

After a while of chatting, drinking coffee, and laughing a lot, we decided that we were hungry. Gert told us about this buffet-style restaurant that was in front of the hotel; we would not even have to get out of the parking lot. This sounded great to us, so we decided to do that. We put Gert in the car (it was too far to push her) and drove to the front of the restaurant.

We were pleased with the selection of food that they had. We got our food, but Gert had already eaten before we got there and said she did not want to eat, so she had some iced tea. We ate, and then when it came time for dessert, Gert decided to partake of that. (Girl after my own heart.) Not long after that, we decided to return to the room for a while. So off we went again.

After returning to the room, we got comfortable and did more talking. Around 10:00 p.m., we called John to come and pick up Gert. We would meet again tomorrow when we got up and got it all together. We were kind of talked out and needed to sleep. It had been a full day.

Wednesday, October 17, 2001

Theresa and I woke up to a knock on the door. It was John, and he was here with doughnuts for us. What a wonderful thing. We love doughnuts. From now on, he would be our doughnut man. He gave us the doughnuts and left with a "See you later." We made coffee and washed up, brushed our teeth, and sat down to have a wonderful meal. This is great; we didn't even have to leave the room.

Theresa was really tired from the three days of travel, and I was not doing too well from two days of driving either. Our ages were looming their ugly heads again. This is why we like to travel at our leisure. Sometimes, we cannot go like we would want too. We have to make allowances for our ages and medical problems.

We decided that we would call Gert to come over after we had woken up good and just spend the day here. We could have some food delivered later if we didn't feel like going out.

Gert called around 11:00 to see if we wanted to go to lunch, we told her that we really weren't hungry. We are not used to eating three meals a day. We usually do two. We had eaten doughnuts and probably would not be hungry till suppertime. We told her that we wanted her to come spend the day with us. That way, we could take photos and just hang out and bore each other. She agreed to this and told us that her daughter, Dianne, would bring her over.

When they arrived, we invited Dianne to stay for a while. She did for a time but then had to leave, saying that she would return later.

Theresa and I had brought little gifts for Gert, and we got them out and gave them to her. She was touched. We chatted for most of the afternoon. We had bought Cokes, juice, and some snacks at the little store we had called her from the day before, and I went and got some ice, so we were well fixed for a day of talking. You know how woman are. They can talk all day and all night and still have more to talk about.

Gert told us that we had made believers of John and her by showing up to visit with her. Others had told her that they were going to visit and then never followed through on it. She was really thrilled. We had a wonderful day. Gert said that John wanted to take us to visit the Morrow Building and the Cowboy Hall of Fame. She wanted us to meet her brother also. So we said that we would do that tomorrow. This made her happy. She felt like she had to entertain us. We tried to explain to her that we did not come to see the sights but to visit her. We got over that entire sightseeing stuff when we were raising our children. However, we would love to visit the Morrow Building Memorial. This is where a terrorist named McVey bombed the building in protest over the Waco fiasco. The Morrow Building was a government building that had many people working in it. It even had a day care center for the worker's children. Many lives were lost, even the poor innocent children. It was an American tragedy. We, Americans, have been so protected. We have not experienced the horrors of war as they had in

Europe and Asia. Now, all of a sudden, we were faced with terrorism. It was a whole new way of life for us. In my opinion, I was not going to let these people make me live in fear of the unknown. I would not take any chances out of the ordinary, but I would live my life the way I saw fit.

We had a scary moment when Gert had to use the restroom. We had trouble getting the wheelchair on the other side of the room to the bathroom. Then, she had to get up, and we had to help her maneuver her way into the small bathroom. She almost lost her balance several times. We had a handicapped room, but it was still not what she was used to at home. We ended up laughing at our antics, but we got the job done.

Around 6:00 p.m., Dianne returned. She offered to go get us something to eat, so we decided that we wanted fried chicken. We were on vacation, and we could eat that fried, fattening, greasy food if we wanted too. Gert called in the order, and Dianne went to get it. Naturally, they did not send all of it, so Gert got back on the phone, and Dianne got back in the car and went to get the rest of it. Never a dull moment!

After we ate our fill, we decided that we would take some photos of all of us. We had a blast, just cutting up taking pictures. You would think we were back in our second childhood. We had a grand time.

Sometime later, we decided to call it a night, so Gert and Dianne left. Gert would call us in the morning to see what time we wanted to go out to see the sights.

Thursday, October 18, 2001

We got up, made coffee, and ate the rest of the doughnuts. Of course, Theresa had her orange juice also. I was taking my shower when Gert called to see what time we wanted to leave, so Theresa told her in about an hour or so. Gert said that she and John would be over to get us.

When they arrived, we were ready. So, we piled into the backseat of their car and off we went with John as chauffer. I really enjoyed this; I was usually the designated driver. It is so much easier because John knew exactly where we were going and how to get there.

Upon reaching the Morrow Building, John told us that he would prefer to stay in the car if we thought we could handle pushing Gert in her wheelchair. We had no problem with this.

You know that we were so lucky; we were able to park directly across from the building, so we did not have to walk very far. (We kept telling you that someone is watching out for us, are you beginning to believe now?)

John got Gert's wheelchair out of the trunk and helped her to get into it. We took over then. We wheeled her across the street. Before going into the memorial, we stopped to look at the Memorial Wall. This is where people put flowers to remember the ones who where lost that day. It is very moving. There are photos of some of them, along with the flowers and teddy bears for the children. We decided that we needed to take some photos of this, so we did. (We love to take photos so we will have them to look back on after the trip is over. You will discover this about us as we go along.)

Once our photos of the wall were taken, we went into the building. Thank the Lord, they have handicapped walkways so we could push Gert's wheelchair up it. We quickly discovered that it was easier to pull the chair up backwards than it was to push it forward.

Oklahoma Memorial Chairs

This opens up to a large courtyard, which has a huge reflection pool in the middle, with all of the memorial chairs for each one lost on one side and the large survivor tree on the other with memorials on each end. The serene aura of this place is overwhelming at first. All of this was very moving, and we walked around in silence at first. Silently praying for this to never happen again and for the lost souls.

After a while, we started to talk, and you guessed it. We took more pictures. We were lucky enough that another tourist took some photos of all of us with our cameras. This was wonderful. We could all three be together. We, of course, did the same for them. We stayed there for about an hour and a half, then decided we had seen enough, and we should not keep John waiting any longer.

When we got back to the car, John was happy to see us. We got Gert back in the car and her chair into the trunk, and we were off to the Cowboy Museum. Poor John, stuck with three chattering women. Good thing he tunes us out. The reason we know that he does this, is because Gert was always telling him how to drive, and he paid no attention to her even though she was sitting next to him and poking him at the same time.

When we arrived at the museum, it was closed. Not willing to make it a nothing stop, I got out and took photos of the outside of the building and the cowboy statue in front. We never did find out why the place was closed. It wasn't a holiday that we knew of.

Gert decided that she wanted us to meet her Brother. So John drove us to his place of business. When we got there, he wasn't there. We were doing really well at this point. The secretary told Gert that he would be back soon, so we decided to wait for him in the car for a while. I needed a cigarette break anyway, so I stood outside and smoked while we all waited.

Not too long after, Gert's brother, Roy, showed up. He was very happy to see us. We had a very nice time talking with him. He, like us, had been to Ireland, and we talked about this to him. We enjoyed our visit with him.

When we left from there, we decided to go back to the motel. We stopped on the way at a Subway and got us something to take back with us to eat. This worked out great for us. That way we would not have to go out again for supper. With this accomplished, we returned to the room.

Of course, John had had enough of us, so he decided that he would leave Gert with us and return for her later. After he left, we realized that we had not taken any photos of him with Gert. We would do this in the morning before we left to go back to Louisiana.

We ate and naturally talked for a good while before Dianne came for Gert. We wanted to get a good night's rest for our trip back. We would stop at Marshall, Texas, again and spend the night. We would get to Houma on Saturday, and on Sunday, we would take another day of rest before going to Theresa's brother. She would spend the next few days with him before returning home.

Friday, October 19, 2001

We got up and did the usual, drank coffee and took showers. In general, we were trying to wake up. I, of course, had to have my morning cigarette. Did I tell ya'll, this is a no-smoking unit and every time I wanted one of the evil things, I had to go outside to do it? This was not very easy on me as it was very chilly this time of year and there had been brisk winds ever since we arrived. Anyway, I would endure all of this for my cigarettes. It was very noticeable that I was not smoking as much on this trip as usual.

We had to finish packing and call Gert. We would stop at her house on the way out. Dianne was going to lead us to the way out of town. This was great since we had gotten lost on the way in.

After we finished packing, we called Gert and told her we would be about another half hour before arriving at her home. We still had to check out of the hotel. We knew this would not take long.

We had no problem with this and were on our way very soon.

When we arrived at Gert's house, we were welcomed by a gaggle of cats. You have never seen so many cats. They were all over the place. They were every color, shape, and size. Naturally, Gert knew every one of them by name.

John was there to hug us good-bye and pose for some photos with Gert. We did not want to stay too long, so we did not lollygag around. We did the bonding stuff, you know, hugs and tears. They had wanted us to stay a few more days, but we really had to be on our way. Theresa was still concerned about her brother but knew that he was doing OK. She had talked to him every day since she had seen him on Saturday.

We got in our car, and Dianne and Gert got in John's car to lead us out of Oklahoma City on our way to Dallas. Once we got on the highway, we would be fine.

Well, we are here to tell you that you should not follow Dianne. She drives very fast. Apparently, she took a few wrong turns, and we could see Gert giving her "what for." When we got to where Dianne was supposed to leave us, she almost missed the exit and almost ran into the barrier. What a scare she gave us! As we passed them, we could see Gert giving it to her again.

Theresa and I were on the road again. We both gave a sigh of relief when we saw the Dallas sign, knowing that this meant we were pointed in the right direction. We had made arrangements to stay in Marshall, Texas, at the same place we stayed in on the way to Oklahoma.

Well, we ran into construction on the way to Dallas. It was a mess, but then, when isn't road construction a mess? We eventually made our way to Dallas and were on our way to Marshall. This was a great relief to us both. The rest of the trip to Marshal was uneventful. We were getting a little anxious because it was starting to get dark and we do not like to drive in the dark.

We made it to Marshall and checked in; then we went to the buffet restaurant that we had been to earlier in the week. We knew that they would have many different things, and we could get a good meal there at a reasonable price. Naturally, we always let them know that we were seniors and wanted our discount. We had a nice meal and returned to the room. Aw, I could smoke in this room, and I was enjoying that.

We had just finished our showers and getting ready for bed when the phone rang. It was Gert. She was calling to let us know that Theresa's brother, Dick, had been rushed back to the hospital. He was having a lot of pressure in his head, and they had to relieve it. Gert gave us the room number that he was supposed to be in at East Jefferson Hospital in New Orleans and the phone number. It seems that they had been trying to reach us since about noon, but we had been on the road, so they had called Gert. We had left our itinerary with Roy and Marvis when we left. We always do this just in case we are needed.

Theresa was very upset and had to calm down some before she could call and check on him. Finally, she was able to call. She talked to her nephew Mike. He said that his father was doing fine now but that he had really given them a bad scare. She asked if we should just get back in the car and drive straight to New Orleans. Mike assured her that he was in no danger at the moment and for us to get a good night's sleep, and then we could check on him to see if we needed to go directly to see if before going to Peg's house.

We would not sleep much tonight. We were both concerned about Dick and wishing that we had not taken an extra day in Oklahoma City at this point, but we could not go back. We had to get what sleep we could so that we could finish our trip tomorrow. We would check with Mike on the way in to see if we needed to head for New Orleans or go to Houma as we had originally planned.

Saturday, October 19, 2001

When we got up in the morning, the first thing we did was get the coffee started and call to see how Dick was. He was doing much better. We told them that we would check with them later in the day.

After driving awhile, we decided to stop for gas and food. This is a necessary evil for all motor vehicles and humans. We stopped at what was advertised as a well-known restaurant. Well, we got our gas and then proceeded to order some food. This is when we realized that this was not a full-service restaurant and the food was not of the quality we were accustomed to. What a disappointment that was. We had stopped there because of that. Oh well, the best-laid plans of mice and men.

When we were paying for a few souvenirs that we had chosen, we saw the lapel American flags. We were thrilled. Both of us had been looking for these. So we added them to our purchases. Lots of people had been wearing these and displaying the flag since the September 11 tragedy. It was American's way of giving support to our government during this dark period.

When we got close to Lafayette, Louisiana, we called Mike again to see how his father was doing. He was improving and in no danger. We decided at this point that we would go on to Houma and then to the hospital in New Orleans on Sunday.

Theresa was quite relieved to hear good news of her brother. She had been very tense since last night when we got the news that he was not doing well.

We were making great time on the road and figured that we may be able to make five o'clock Mass at St. Louis Church on the way home. This was the Mass that I usually went to, and we would not have to worry about it in the morning. We could just make the trip to New Orleans to see Dick. This was a blessing to us, and we wanted to thank God for taking very good care of us on this trip and for watching over Dick. We had much to be thankful for.

We walked into the church just as the priest was entering the altar. Luckily, we were able to sit with Roy. He was there, as was his custom on Saturdays, also. He was very surprised to see us. He had not expected us till later.

After church, we went to my house and we called to check on Dick again. We told Mike that if we were needed, we would be here until tomorrow when we would go to New Orleans. Theresa felt much better about being only an hour away from her brother.

Needless to say, we unloaded the car, ate, got on the computer for a short time, and then got some sleep.

Sunday, October 20, 2001

Upon getting up, we had our coffee, juice, and some breakfast. Then we started to plan the day out. We would check on Dick and decided what time we would leave for New Orleans.

Theresa had planned to spend the last few days of her visit at Dick's; however, this would not be a good time for that now, so we decided that she would stay with me, and we would go to see Dick as often as we could till she had to leave for Maine. Once this was decided, we both seemed to breathe a little easier.

Around noon, just before we were ready to leave for New Orleans, Mia, my daughter, called. She had a problem and wondered if we would help her out. It seemed she just was called into work and had no one to care for Jordan. We told her that we were on our way to the city and, if she could get his nanny to take him for a few hours, that we could pick him up there and then take him back to Slidell for her and spend the night. This worked wonderful for her. Mia works in St. Rose, at a lab now. (Oh, we forgot to tell you, she finally finished college and had her degree in chemistry and microbiology.) She told us that she would drop Jordan at his nanny's and that they would go to church around the time we would be visiting with Dick so we could just pick him up at the nursery at church. If we had any problems, we would call and let them know. Jordan's nanny is named Teresa; she is the head RN for a hospital just outside of New Orleans. We had her home number and cell phone number so we could keep in touch with her and let her know what time we would pick him up. That way, we would not be driving all over Kenner to find him.

We packed a few things for our overnight stay and then took off for New Orleans to see Dick. We went straight to the hospital to see him. East Jefferson Hospital is a large hospital. We had to get someone to show us how to get to his room, plus a wheelchair for Theresa. We knew that she could not walk that far without stopping several times to rest, so we had a wheelchair for her. We do this whenever we feel that it is too much for either one of us. We are seniors, not stupid.

When we got to Dick's room, he wasn't there. We were told that he was having physical therapy and would return soon. We waited.

Dick and Marvis were delighted when they returned to the room to find us waiting for them. Dick looked very weak but good to us. He told us of how he realized that something was wrong and how Marvis had insisted that he go to the emergency room to be checked out and how he was readmitted to the hospital. He had quite a scare. When told that he would have to go back into surgery to relieve the pressure, he was at the point where he just wanted relief. He said he felt like his head was ready to explode.

Theresa explained to Dick and Marvis that she would spend the rest of her vacation at my house because she felt that they had enough to deal with at this time. This way, she could come and visit him, and I would take her to the airport when the time came for her to return home. Dick and Marvis were relieved about this. They told us that they had wondered how Marvis could be a good hostess and still be at the hospital at the same time. We spent a few hours with them and then decided to go pick up Jordan. We did not want to tire Dick out too much, and he had been through quite an ordeal in the last few days. We said our good-byes and left.

I deposited Theresa and the wheelchair in the front of the hospital and then went to the parking garage to get the car. We could not see the sense of Theresa having to make that long walk again.

When we checked with Teresa, we found out that Jordan was at the church nursery, and she was in the church. She told us that she had told them to let her know when we arrived so that she could give us her car seat for him. (She was not aware that I already had a car seat for my grandkids in the backseat of my car that stays there for whenever I need it.) This was great; we were not too far from there.

When we arrived at the nursery, Jordan was sound asleep. We hated to wake him, so we thought if we waited a little while that he would wake up. Teresa came, and we talked for a while. Theresa had never met Teresa, so this was a good chance for them to meet since they both knew of each other. Jordan had told his nanny, Teresa, about his friend Theresa from Maine and vice versa. So they felt like they knew each other.

We decided that it was time to wake Jordan; we did not want to drive to Slidell too late. As ya'll know, we don't like to drive when it starts to get dark.

Jordan was happy to see all of us together. He had to hug and kiss everyone. (He is going to be a ladies' man). We said our good-byes to Teresa and the nursery worker, and off we went to Slidell. (Slidell is an hour's drive east of New Orleans.) Before we got to Mia's, we decided that we would stop and get us some food to take there that way we would not have to worry about it later. We stopped at a Chinese place that I knew about not far from Mia's and ordered enough food for all four of us. We were set now. We had Jordan, food, and a place to sleep.

When we got to Mia's, I called her at work and let her know that we had already picked up Jordan and that we were at the house with enough food for all. She was happy to hear from us. We told her not to worry, that we were all fine, and would be eating in a few minutes. She told us that she would be there as soon as she had the results of the experiment that she was doing. This would take a few more hours; you just can't rush those things and expect them to come out right.

After we ate, we played with Jordan for a while outside. (Mia has a play yard for him, with just about every outside toy that you can think of.) After about an hour or so, we took him back into the house. He wanted to stay outside, but it was getting dark.

About 8:00 p.m., we got on the computer to let everyone know that we had seen Dick that day and that their prayers were working. Never underestimate the power of prayer. The doctors are great, but sometimes, you need help from a higher power.

Mia arrived home about 9:00 p.m. She thanked us for helping her out and having some food for her to eat. Mia loves Chinese food like we do, so this was a treat for her. We talked for a while, and then we realized that we were both dog tired and needed our sleep. It had been several days since either of us had had a good night's sleep.

Monday, October 21, 2001

Well, Theresa and I were both dragging when we got up, so we decided that we would rest today if Dick was doing OK. When we checked on Dick, we found out that he was doing really good. So, Theresa told him that we would call him later that day to see how he was progressing. This was a relief to both of us. We would spend the day in Slidell, and then on the way back to Houma tomorrow, we would stop at the hospital to see Dick. We needed a day of rest. You know, when you don't have to do anything. Mia was dropping Jordan off at his nursery school on her way to work, so we would have the house to ourselves. This was perfect. We would pick up Jordan in the afternoon for Mia. This would save her time and a few miles, and Jordan loves when his granny picks him up.

We want you to know that we did nothing this day but rest. I thought about us going to see my friend Lucille in Picayune, Mississippi (which was about thirty-five miles away), but we decided against it. We even thought of going to the casino and gambling for a while, but we were just too tired to even do that. Boy, that doesn't happen often, that we give up a chance like that. Will wonders never cease! We called Roy and let him know that we would not be back today so that he would not worry about us. He has a habit of doing this. He thinks that we need protection (from ourselves mainly).

About 5:00 p.m., we went and picked up Jordan, and he had to introduce his Teesa to all of his friends and teachers. They told her that he talks of her often. Mia arrived home not long after we did, so we all fixed supper and chatted. Jordan was in his glory, playing the drums for his Teesa and hugging her every time he got the chance. Naturally, I took photos of all of this for posterity.

We watched a little TV and then went to the computer. We had to report in. We got on the computer and reported our day to our chat-room buddies. They wanted to hear what kind of mischief we were up too. They were shocked to learn that we had been good girls that day and had not gotten into any situations for them to laugh about. I think that they were disappointed. Soon after, we all went to bed.

Tuesday, October 22, 2001

When we got up, Mia and Jordan were already gone. We had told Jordan that we would be leaving in the morning, and he had thrown a fit. He didn't want us to leave. He cried and carried on for a while, but he came to realize that we must go. The reason that we did this is because if we don't tell him and he comes home and finds us gone, he really gives Mia a lot of trouble. He gets mad at her and will not speak to her and will do that that all children do to let you know that they are not happy.

We drank our coffee and juice and ate some toast. We called and told Dick and Marvis that we would be stopping by to visit with him in about two hours and asked if there was anything that we could bring them. They told us, "Yes, bring yourselves." How sweet!

We had a nice trip back to the city. Traffic was not as heavy as usual. I deposited Theresa in front of the hospital and proceeded to the parking garage to park the car. When I returned, I found her sitting in a wheelchair already. Boy, she was on the ball today. Then we proceeded to Dick's room.

When we got there, Dick and Marvis were all excited. The doctor had just told them that they could go home in a few hours after Dick's therapy session.

We visited for an hour or so and then left for Houma. After we were back for a while, we lay down for a while. We decided to do our laundry; that way Theresa would have fresh clothes for the rest of the week and would not have to go to the Laundromat till the next week. Roy came in to check and see if we had arrived back home and to see what our plans were for the rest of the day. We were happy to say that we were going to cook dinner, do the laundry, and just lie around the house the rest of the day. We told him that we wanted to go back to see Dick the next morning and then go to the casino for a few hours before coming back to Houma. He was all for this. He likes to gamble as much as we do. So, he agreed to go with us. Theresa would be leaving early Thursday morning, so this would be her last visit with Dick and Marvis, and she was ready to go to the casino. We just know that the city of Kenner would not survive if we did not contribute to their coffers by our donations. Right, playing penny machines.

That night, all of my kids came over to visit with us. This was good. Theresa loves the grandkids and always makes a big deal when she sees them. Of course, Roy and I do the same all the time.

Wednesday, October 23, 2001

After Theresa and I got up, we did the usual, and then Roy came in to check on us. He was going to wake us up if we weren't up so that we could leave to go to visit Dick and go to the casino. (Roy is an early riser, about 5:00 a.m.) He was glad to see that we were up and moving. Hehehe! We told him that we would be ready in about an hour. This made him happy; we would get to Dick's before noon. Theresa called Dick and told him that we would be there in about two hours. Dick was happy that we would come see him today. Theresa would be leaving tomorrow morning around 6:00 a.m., so this would be the last chance he would have to see her for some time.

When we arrived at Dick and Marvis, they were waiting for us. We visited for about two hours, and then, we were off to the casino. Theresa, Dick, and Marvis had a teary farewell, and Theresa told them that she would call that night to say good-bye.

Needless to say, we did not make a killing at the casino. We donated to the economy of the city of Kenner. This makes everyone but us happy. We did enjoy our time there though. On the way home, as usual, I was kicking myself for doing it.

We got home before 6:00 p.m. Theresa still had a little packing left to do, and naturally, I was giving her stuff to take home for her to eat. I gave her some jars of green beans from the garden. She loves Roy's green beans, and we had gotten some creole gumbo and jambalaya mix for her to take home. After finishing her packing, we had supper, did the dishes, and got on the computer to talk to our cyber friends.

We would have to be up around 3:00 a.m. It takes an hour to get to the airport from here. Since the terrorist attack on the WTC, they had beefed up security at the airports, so you had to report in two hours before your scheduled flight. We went to bed early for us, not for Roy, so that we could get some sleep for tomorrow. Theresa needed her sleep; she would have a long day ahead of her.

Thursday, October 24, 2001

Well, here it was, 3:00 a.m., and we were headed to the airport. I can't believe I was moving at this hour. I was usually just going to sleep at this time.

It was a little foggy on the way to the airport but not as bad as we thought it might be. We didn't have any problems getting there, so we were there early.

In fact, we were there so early that when we stopped at the entrance to put her luggage down, there were no skycaps to help. There were also no wheelchairs outside, so I went in to get one while Roy waited with Theresa at the curb.

It took me awhile to find someone to even talk too, let alone get a wheelchair from. This finally accomplished, I returned to Theresa and Roy outside. I pushed Theresa in, and Roy brought her luggage in, and then he went to park the car. There was still no one at the ticket counter for Theresa to check in with. Some security. Why did they insist that we get there so early if they weren't going to have anyone there to check you in? There were several others in the same fix that we were, and they were about as happy with it as we were.

Finally, about ten to five, they had people to check you through. We did this and were informed at that time that due to new security measures, we could not go to the gate with Theresa. They assured me that they would have someone to take her there and help her on the plane. Somehow, this did not warm my heart. We stayed with Theresa until they came to take her to the gate. We said our good-byes, and then we left the airport. There was no sense in us staying there and not being able to be with her till it was time to board the plane. Theresa promised that she would call when she arrived home, so I had to be satisfied with that. She only had one stopover to make, and the airlines would have someone to get her to the next gate. The reason I worried about her is she was so lenient with everything and everyone. She would sit there and not complain even if she thought she would miss her plane. She figures that they would get her there on time. This does not always happen, the way it is supposed too. When we got back home, I was tired out from the trip, so I lay back down while Roy went out to tend to his field.

Around noon, Roy came in, and we had dinner. Not too long after, Theresa called to say that she was home, so I could stop worrying. We did not stay on the phone long. We would talk tonight on the computer with our friends.

Bye, see ya'll next trip!

The Land of the Golf Carts

Well, here we are again, on our way to the airport to pick up Theresa. Needless to say, it is raining. Does it ever do anything else when she is coming here? We are planning to leave for Florida the day after tomorrow.

We are going to see our Internet friends, Bill and Vera. We also will be stopping at my sister's in Bradenton, two of my uncles (one in Port St. Lucie and the other in New Port Richey. All are near Tampa. From there, we will be going to my brother Dick's place on the eastern side of Florida, in Edgewater. So, we will have full days. But then, what else is there for us but full days.

When we arrived at the airport, we went to her gate and found Theresa's brother, Dick, waiting as always. He always meets her when he can, and then we spend some time with him and Madres (his wife) at his house before going to Houma. Well, wonder of wonders, her plane is on time in spite of the weather. There she is, full of smiles. Riding in a wheelchair, looking like a queen.

We spent the weekend at Peg's, where we did nothing but eat and sleep and visit. We were leaving on Monday morning, and we wanted to be bright eyed and bushy tailed for the trip to Florida. We had quite a few people to visit there.

Monday morning, with Roy's help, we loaded up the car. Once that was done, we said our good-byes and were off. Being on the open road again was great. We enjoy each other's company, and that is a plus.

It looked as if we were going to have an uneventful trip, but fate stepped in.

We were driving to Tallahassee, where we would spend the night. Just before getting there, the car started to pull to the right. I thought, *Oh no.* I figured there was something wrong with the right front tire. So, I stopped to check it on the side of the road. Much to my horror, I was right. The tire was peeling. We decided to try to make it to the motel that we were staying at for the night, and we could have it fixed. We could ask them at the motel who to call.

When we arrived at the motel and checked in. They told us that Wal-Mart was just two blocks away that had the garage facilities. We were thrilled, and it was quite a relief. Now we just had to get the car there, without any mishap, like a blowout or the tire just peeling down to nothing.

When we went to the room, we discovered a whole lot of state police cars and men. We decided to talk to them about the car and see what they thought. They agreed with us that we would probably need a new tire, and Wal-Mart was probably the best and cheapest place for us to go. They told us they were there for a law enforcers' convention and, if any of them could help us, just to let them know. We told them the only problem we could foresee would be if we could not make it to the Wal-Mart. They told us if we just nursed the car along like we did to get there, we would probably be fine. From their mouth to God's ears. Anyway, we talked with a few of them for over an hour before going to our room. They helped us take our luggage to the room. That was so nice of them. Not too often when you find gentlemen in the area.

After we were in the room for a while, we decided to order in because we did not want to use the car till we absolutely had too. So we ordered a pizza, a Hawaiian one. I had never had one of those, and I figured I might as well try it. Theresa said it was good. After taking our showers and getting ready for bed, we ate some pizza. Then we read for a while till we were sleepy. Then we went to sleep.

When we got up the next morning, it was early. We dressed and then checked out of the motel and headed to Wal-Mart. We drove very slow to Wal-Mart to have the tire fixed. We were very lucky we were second in line. It turned out that we would need a new tire for the right front, so I told them to change the left front also. They did this in a timely manner, we were pleased with their work. So we took off on our way to a little below Tampa. We were going to the home of Bill and Vera. Two of the wonderful buddies that we had formed a friendship with in the chat room we frequently went to. Bill called us when we were on the interstate, but Theresa did not know how to answer the cell phone; I had only learned recently. So when we got to a rest stop, we pulled in. We took care of nature's call; then we called Bill. He wanted to check in with us and see how far we had progressed, so he could gage when we would be arriving at his house. It made us feel good that he was checking on us. Bill gave us directions to his house so that made us feel better. Now we knew where we were supposed to go. Plus my daughter called while we were there to see how we were doing. We told her of our tire trouble of the day before and how we had run into the whole State of Florida state trooper force, and she laughed and told us it would only happen to us.

When we reached Bill and Vera's, there was a guard gate, so we had to wait till they called them to OK our entrance into their world. When we got to their home, they were outside waiting for us, with hugs and welcomes. We were glad to see them too and thankful that we could stand for a while. Sitting all day in the car, we wanted to stand for a while.

We were supposed to spend tonight and tomorrow night, then go on to one of the uncles for an overnight visit. He only lived two hours away.

It was Bill's birthday, and we had come to celebrate with him. He suggested that we go out to eat, but Theresa and I asked if we could just eat in tonight and go out to eat tomorrow because we were really tired. Being the good host that he was, he agreed. I dug in my bag and pulled out the hostess gift that I had made for them. I had embroidered two dresser scarves for them. They really liked them. I told them that dinner was on us tomorrow in celebration of Bill's birthday. Bill kind of frowned but didn't say no.

Bill ordered something for us to eat and then went to pick it up. When he got back, we were ready to eat. We were starved. We ate and talked awhile. Then we started to get showers and get ready for bed. After that, Bill and I talked on the Lanai while the others went to bed. He talked about his love for Vera. It was wonderful to know that this kind of love still existed. It made me realize that I cared for Roy in the same way.

Bill and I talked half the night about our friends in the chat room. How I loved to quilt and embroider, and he loved to cross stitch. He had asked me for my favorite picture from our Ireland trip, and I had sent him a picture of Connamore Castle. He had cross stitch it on to a mat and had it framed. To this day, it hangs in my bedroom where I can see it every day. It is one of my treasured possessions. You know when you meet people in chat rooms, you never think that you will actually met them, much less become friends. It seems like that this happened with most of us in this room. What a plus, they had all been to my life. I guess when you get to be our age, things change. Some things that were important to you when you were younger don't matter any longer, and others seem so much more important.

When we couldn't hold our eyes open any longer, we bid each other good night and went to bed.

In the morning, we got up all bright eyed and bushy tailed and were ready to face the world. And when we faced it, it looked pretty good.

We were at a friend's home, and they had cooked breakfast. Theresa got her orange juice. (As long as she has her orange juice, she is happy.) I had coffee. Then we had a great breakfast, and naturally, we sat around and talked. That evening, we decided what restaurant Bill wanted to go to for his birthday dinner. He was all tickled; he said no one ever drove that far to take him to feed him. We all laughed. Bill liked to joke a lot, and he was good at it. We decided that we would leave for the restaurant around 4:30 p.m. That way, we would be there before they got their rush at 6:00 p.m. Anyway, that is what we thought.

When we arrived it was not too crowded, and we got a table right away. We let our waitress know that it was Bill's birthday without him being aware of it. About halfway through dinner, my colitis kicked in, and I was off to the bathroom. I was in there it seemed like forever. I know that it wasn't, but it seemed like that. Theresa even came to check on me once.

Finally, I was able to return to the table. I asked the waitress if she would just box my food to go; I knew that I wouldn't eat anything else now. A few minutes later, a bunch of the servers headed our way, clapping their hands and singing "Happy Birthday" to Bill, and brought a small cake for him. He was thrilled. He didn't realize that we had had it done, and he didn't catch us doing it. We all laughed at his antics. Vera was enthralled. She cared so much for this man of hers that she was as happy for him as he was. When we got back to the house, we got on the computer for a while. We wanted to let our friends know that we had made it to Bill's in one piece. They were glad to know this. They all worry about us when we are on one of these trips. It's funny how close you can get to someone you have never seen. That is how it is with our group. God love them all.

Well, it was time to go to bed; we had to hit the road tomorrow. We would be on our way to my uncle Jack's and aunt Ginny's. It had been several years since I had seen them, so I was looking forward to it.

We did not have any problems getting there. We were happy that we did not have far to go to get there. My uncles are very special to me, and now with all of us scattered all over the country, it is hard to see them. We keep in touch through e-mail, but it's not the same thing. There is nothing like a McCue hug. We had a great time talking on their screened porch. Theresa could not get over that everyone there uses their golf carts like a second car. They even have a special lane for them on the highways in town. Uncle Jack kept us laughing as always. We were really enjoying our selves. They, to surprise us, had wanted to cook here for us. We had wanted to take them out. Anyway, we had a great meal. After supper and the dishes were done, we did some more talking.

I was planning to go see my sister who lived about thirty minutes away in the morning, so I wanted to get a good night's sleep. Sis always keeps us hopping; we never know for sure where or when she will pop up. Uncle Jack said he wanted to talk about my visiting her. I knew what was coming next. He said, "I know you love your sister, but you know how she drains you. Peg, you can't give her any money. Promise me that you will not let her get to you." He was right, and I know that I can't keep passing her money, but she was special, and I had a hard time refusing her. That is another story, and right now, I am not going there. Anyway, I promised my uncle that I would try to do what he asked.

The next morning, we woke up and had breakfast and got ready to leave. It is always hard saying good-bye, so it took a few minutes longer than we thought.

When we got down the road a ways, Theresa and I got to talking about what we were going to face with my sister. Theresa kept telling me that everything would be all right. We found the motel all right. I told them I was expecting some guest, so they could just direct them to our room.

Well, to my surprise, they had already arrived and were waiting for us.

There was my sister, Sis, her daughter, Alice, and son, Henry. I was hoping that I would have a few minutes to collect myself after the drive. That was not going to happen. So, Theresa opened the door, and every one took a bag from the trunk and brought it in. We sat down to chat for a while. When the sun started setting, I asked Alice where was a good place for all of us to go have something to eat. She told me there were several in the area. I told her to pick a place that Sis liked. So, she did. We all piled in my car, and off we went. When we got to the restaurant, Alice pulled me to the side and told me that neither she nor Sis had money to pay for anything. I told her not to worry about it. I would take care of it. When we sat down at the table, Sis grabbed the menu. She cannot read, but she can write beautifully. She can copy them. She can tell which things are the most expensive, and she loves ordering that. We ordered, and then we ate. We had a nice meal. I was thrilled because Sis seemed like she was on her best behavior. After supper, we went back to the room. Alice told me that they could not stay long because she had to work in the morning. Sis went into her usual mode asking all sorts of questions. Things that had been answered a long time ago, but she could not let go. Theresa and Alice ended up referees before they left. Sis told me that she would be back in the morning to wish us good-bye. We did not tell her that we were going to Uncle Bill's.

Uncle Jack and Uncle Bill did not want her to know how really close they lived to her because they could not take the drama. She, as usual, asked me for some money; this was not unexpected. I had already given Alice some money for her to get her something when I was gone. I asked her how much she needed. She told me a hundred. I told her that I didn't have that much. I could let her have $25, but that was it.

She said, "Can you make it $50 'cause there is a shorts set that I want, and that would buy it." So I told her to let me think about it, and I would let her know in the morning.

View from Uncle Bill's Bird

Well, as you can figure, she was at our door bright and early. We got some coffee and juice and toast and ate. Then we started to get ready to leave. I was glad to know that Theresa was in the room when I took my shower, so Sis could not go through my things. She had already asked me for my shawl, and I had told her that I would make her one and mail it to her. That seemed to satisfy her. After we carried out the luggage, I sat down and told her I love her and gave her the $50. She was thrilled. Theresa and I were thrilled to leave without any drama. We left Sis and Henry waving us good-bye. We were off to Uncle Bill's in New Port Lucy.

When we arrived at Uncle Bill's, he had been waiting for us. He had a snack and some iced tea waiting for us. That was so nice of him. He told us that we would be going out for supper but that we would go around 4:00 or 4:30. He said because all the old people go for 5:00. We laughed and told him that we were "the old people."

There was a knock at his door; he peeked to see who it was and told us, "Oh Lord, it's my neighbor. You have to protect me. She's been after me since Aunt Murph died. I have a girlfriend now, and she still won't leave me alone." We started laughing, and he answered the door. She told him, "Bill, are you OK? I saw two ladies in your drive, and they were strange looking, so I wanted to come check on you." He told her "Jane, come in and met the strange ladies. This is my niece and her friend, Peggy and Theresa."

Well, Jane looked like she swallowed her tongue. We had all we could do to keep a straight face. She was checking on him to see if one of us was there for him. We chatted for a few minutes, and then she left, but not without inviting herself to go out with us for dinner. After she left, Uncle Bill told us how she was always after him. He told us she even follows him to the pool when he takes his swim every day. It's not like he doesn't have a girlfriend because he does.

Only she was out of town right now and would not be back for two more weeks.

We decided to take a little walk around the subdivision. When we walked outside, the pond, which is directly to the right of his house, was beautiful. There was a bird in one of the trees growing out of the water. I am not sure what kind of bird it was, but it was so beautiful that I had to go to the car and take a picture of it. It just looked so peaceful there. We did take our walk after we marveled at the bird and the serenity that it made us feel.

Soon, it was time for us to go out to eat. Jane came over to see if we were all ready, and we were. We went out to eat at one of those buffet places that seem to be everywhere in Florida. We did get there before the crowd. It seemed that the rest of the seniors were not far behind us.

After dinner, we went back to the house. It seemed strange for me that Aunt Murph was not there. She was such a dynamic person. Full of life and so funny. She and Uncle Bill were such a great match. I know it had to be hard for him. We decided to play dominos rather than watch television or read. We didn't have to be up early the next morning, so we stayed up a little late. We had a great time.

The next morning when we got up, Uncle Bill had some juice and coffee fixed. Uncle Bill marveled how Theresa seemed to be accepted right away by all my family. She seemed to enjoy them also. I needed to call my friend Cindy; we were supposed to have lunch with her, and we needed to find out how to get to the restaurant. We should put that she was one of those friends that we met online too. She drives a school bus as well as sews for out. She was looking for a certain piece of material, and we found it here in Houma. So I got it and sent it to her. After that, we talk frequently. She told me how to get there, and we set a time that could accommodate her. We packed up the car and told Uncle Bill good-bye. He wanted us to stay. (I think that was so we could protect him from Jane.) We would go to Dick's after lunch with Cindy. Dick lived in Edgewater, all the way on the other side of the state. Well, after we shed all the tears and said our good-byes, we were on our way to meet Cindy. When we got to the restaurant, Cindy was there waiting for us. We talked for a few minutes outside before going into the restaurant. She had reserved a nice table for us. One that we could talk without being overheard. It was really nice.

We ordered our food and got back to talking. After we finished our food, we had about one and a half hours left before Cindy had to go to work. Gotta keep those school buses rolling. Keep those kids learning so they can pay taxes in a few years, so we can keep our Social Security checks coming in.

Now we were on our way to Dick's. I was anxious to see my brother; I hadn't seen him in over two years, and that's too long. We thought about stopping at Disney World, but we really didn't have the time, so we drove on.

Dick had given me explicit directions, so we were fine. Theresa was telling me that she would like to go to St. Augustine because so many of her friends in Maine had told her how beautiful it was. So we decided to stay at Dick's two days instead of three. That way we could stop at St. Augustine without turning our plans into a mess.

When we arrived at Dick's, we had to go through a guard gate to get in. We found the house. Dick was waiting for us; the guard had called him and told him that we had arrived.

We were all happy to see each other. Kathy had not returned from work yet, but she should be here shortly. Blue, the dog, was so happy to see me. He danced all around me. When I sat down, he jumped on my lap. Now this is a sight you need to imagine. Here I am in this nice chair, and I have a 120-pound dog on my lap, kissing me. Dick fussed Blue, and he got down. That was wonderful. Now he lay on the floor, partly on my feet. And I didn't even give him a treat yet.

View from Dick's porch

Kathy came home later, and we all decided that we were going out for Chinese. While Kathy was changing, Theresa and I went out on the back porch. It was so beautiful out there on the porch. We stared at the lake, and then we saw an alligator there. We called Dick and showed him the critter, and he called the clubhouse to tell them about the alligator so they could send someone to catch it and get it out of there. They had had some dogs missing, and this was probably the culprit. Theresa was upset by this; she was afraid that they were going to kill it. When I told her they were just going to catch it and then they would release it somewhere in the swamps like we do in Louisiana, she was all right about it then. Leave it to Theresa; every time she comes south, she attracts alligators. If she comes to my house, the alligators show up, never happens when she is not there. They just swarm to her like men. She has that magnetism for men and alligators.

We went out for dinner, and it was great. We enjoyed the food at the Chinese restaurant. As usual, we could not eat all of it, so we took it home for Blue. When we returned to the house, we were all tired, so we all got ready for bed, bid everyone good night, and went to bed.

The next morning when we got up, Dick told us he wanted to take us to Daytona. There is part of the beach there that you can drive your car on. You can watch the waves roll in on the beach. That was a great idea; we got ready and left.

Dick decided that we should eat before we left town. We stopped at a restaurant that Dick frequented often. We had a nice lunch. Dick talked with a few of his friends that happened to be there.

New Smyrna Beach

The beach was beautiful, and after riding on the beach for a while, we got out and walked on the beach. I was a beautiful sight, and we were glad Dick thought of it. Every time I think of Daytona, I think of the 500. It makes me sad. One of my cousins was killed in the race some years ago. So this was really good; I would now have some good memories to think of about Daytona. We stayed there for a while. He showed us a few more sights on the way back to the house. He took us to see his new boat. It was really nice; I know he will get a lot of use from that. It seems like since he moved to Florida from Pennsylvania, he has more friends that come to visit than he had there. That is typical, they tell me.

Dick had put some stuff in the oven before we left. He checked on it and said that it would be a couple of hours before it was ready. He said he likes to have supper cooked for Kathy, so when she comes home, she does not have to start cooking. Boy, that's great! My husband and I worked the same hours, so I did not have that luxury.

We went out on the porch because it was a great place just to sit. Theresa loved this porch; she just wished she could have one like it. We watched the fish swimming and just enjoyed. I enjoyed so much that I took a nap.

When Kathy got home, she made a great cheese dish for us to snack on. Then we had the roast and potatoes and carrots that Dick had cooked. I was a great meal. While having supper, we asked them where were the best places in St. Augustine. They were full of suggestions, so we made a list of their suggestions. We would be able to refer to them in the morning. We asked Kathy if she would wake us in the morning so that we could get an early start. Dick wanted us to go back there tomorrow night, but we told him that we were just going to start the drive back to home after our sightseeing. If it was too late in the evening, we would just spend the night there and then start out the next day for New Orleans. Theresa was going to spend some time with her brother and Marvis.

What can I say about St. Augustine? It was a great day. We took the Trolley tour and saw the old cannons in the fort. The best thing about this tour was the Fountain of Youth. Yes, I said the Fountain of Youth. I guess it must have worked for us because Theresa and I are still here kicking. Old Ponce de Lyon found this garden and swore that the spring that fed the fountain had marvelous properties. It could make you young again. Well, we are not really young again, but we're not decrepit either. We are still doing our thing.

We decided to go to the Flagler College. They had a tour of the college. It didn't start out as a college, but that is what it is today. The inside is fantastic. The artwork on the ceiling and the walls is breathtaking. Everywhere you look, there was gold on the walls. I mean real gold. They used real gold in the walls and other places. It was fascinating. The tour guides are students of the college and can answer almost any question you ask about Henry Flagler, the man that built all of this as a rest area for millionaires and socialites coming from the north going south and from the south going north. He was the only game in town. It was like a king's palace. It was really awe inspiring. The tour lasted about one and a half hours. By the time we finished these, we were tired. We decided to find us a room for the night.

While looking for a room, we decided to take one more tour. The Savory Faire tour was a food tour. Some of our fellow tourist were telling us about it when we were waiting for the college tour to start. Theresa and I had never done one like this. So we were going to do it. If we didn't like it, we could always leave. Our guide was very friendly, and we really enjoyed him. He took us to seven or eight different restaurants. All different kinds of food from all over the world. We sampled the dishes at each one. I must say most of it was very good. There were all kinds of cuisine. It was really a great tour. We had never taken a tour like this before.

Flagler College

Now we could go to the motel and sleep. We would start for home tomorrow. Well, we were up around 8:00 a.m., so by 9:00, we were ready to leave. I was anxious to see how far we would get. We had been on the road quite a few days, and both of us were getting tired of riding.

We drove along with no problems. Just the way, every one wishes for when they are on a trip. We decided that we would probably stop in Tallahassee; that seemed to be about the midway point. If we did that, we would arrive at the house of Theresa's brother, Dick, in the early afternoon tomorrow. I could rest there a few hours, then drive the hour to Houma and home. We had a very uneventful ride; we stopped for lunch around 1:00 p.m. and stretched our legs. We did that pretty often. I was trying to keep from getting stiff, and so was Theresa. The rest areas on this highway are pretty nice.

We did end up staying in Tallahassee. We checked into a motel, and they had some nice restaurants close by. So we went and ate, and then we got to rest. I had a nice night of sleep and was bright eyed and bushy tailed when I got up. So we were off in no time. On the road again and on our way to our destination. Dick's house in Kenner.

We made it there faster than we thought we would. Traffic was flowing well, and we had no major holdups.

Dick and Marvis were happy to see us. They didn't think we would be there that early. We talked for a while, and then, we said our good-byes. They wanted me to spend the night, but I was only an hour's ride from home, and I was anxious to see Roy and sleep in my own bed tonight.

Well, we made it through, this time with flying colors, and had a grand time doing it. We would look forward to another trip but not for a few months. Bye, see you next time.

St. Augustine oldest living tree (Old Senator)

Our Limo Ride

Well, here I am. Roy is taking me to the airport in Kenner, Louisiana. I am on my way to Portland, Maine. I will be staying at Theresa's. I am going because Theresa and her daughter, Helen, keep telling me that it is my turn to fly. They are having a St. Patrick's party at the club (the Irish American Club) of which Theresa is a member, and every year, they ask me to come for it.

It will also be Helen's birthday a few days before. So we can celebrate that too. The chat-room buddies are planning a dinner at the Willows in Dunellen, New Jersey, on St Patrick's Day and want us to go. We told them, we had the party at the club the night before and we probably would not be able to make it. Theresa and I had not given up on trying to get there. The only thing is that it is a far piece from Falmouth, Maine, to Dunellen, New Jersey.

I had a great flight. No turbulence or nothing that makes your stomach do flip-flops. We had to stop in Philadelphia to take on more passengers, and then off we went on our way to Portland.

We arrived and I went to get my luggage. Theresa always picked me up on the outside of the baggage claims office. Surprise! Helen was waiting for me. She said her mom didn't like driving in snow flurries, so she decided she would pick me up instead.

We talked all the way to the house. I was catching up on Helen's love life. From the way she described it, at the time, it was dull. I told her, "Keep the faith, it will improve." She just laughed. So did I.

Theresa was glad to see us make it to the house but was concerned that Helen would have to drive home. So she promised to go straight home and give her a call when she got there. Theresa was worried until Helen called and said she was home. She told her the snow had stopped, but the radio said it would start again in the morning. Oh happy day! I didn't bring my rubber boots with me. We weren't planning on going out tomorrow anyway.

Theresa had fixed us a snack 'cause she thought that I may be hungry. She was right, I was. So we had a cup of tea and some cheese and crackers. After that, we made up the sofa bed for me, talked awhile, and then we went to bed. I was tired from traveling.

In the morning, I put on a pot of coffee for me. Theresa doesn't drink coffee. Then, I hit the bathroom. Later, when I was having my coffee and toast, Theresa came floating out of her room with a smile on her face. I asked her, "What kind of a dream were you having that you are so happy this early in the morning?" She told me, "No dream, just glad that you are here." How great to have a friend like this.

When I first get up in the morning, I am not the most talkative person; I need time to pull it together. So it usually takes me an hour or so to focus. Theresa is much like me in that respect. So when we were finally ready to talk, we discussed what we were going to do during my time here.

She told me along with her daughter Helen's birthday, she had her sister Helen's birthday and her niece Tina's birthday. The three were all within three days of each other. So I told her, "Well, I had figured that we would take Helen out to eat at a Chinese restaurant, and I would pick up the tab. So we might as well invite them and make it a birthday dinner for all of them." Theresa said she hoped I would say that, but she wanted to pay for half of it. I told her we could discuss that later. We talked about the party at the club. She had reserved our table and ordered our food for it. Naturally, she had chosen the chicken, which was fine with me. She told me that they were having Irish dancers to entertain, and then there would be dancing. Sounded nice.

We talked about going to New Jersey on the seventeenth to meet with our chat-room buddies but did not see how we could swing it because we were going to the Irish dance on the night of the sixteenth. We would love to go to meet these people in person. That way, we would have a face to put with the name. We knew that all of them were not going to be there, but we would still like to meet the ones that would be there. We need to get our brains working to see what we could do about this. Where there is a will, there is a way. That is what I was told since I was a little girl by the nuns. The nuns wouldn't lie. So we had to figure it out. We would love to surprise them and go. We decided to get serious about this, so we looked up to see just how far it was. On the map, it looked to be around six hundred miles. So we thought, maybe we could get a flight from Portland to New York and then rent a car and drive the rest of the way.

We called a couple of airlines to get a price on three round-trip tickets. One for Theresa, one for Helen, and one for me. The price they quoted me was just too much, and then we would have to put a car rental on that too. Helen had to work the next day, so we could not take our time coming back. Then we checked with the railroad to see if Amtrak had a train going there. Of course, they didn't. They would not be too far from it, but we would have to still rent a car along with the train fare, and it was not leaving early enough for it to work for us. Theresa's car could not be trusted on a trip that far. It was a nice car, but old. It wasn't giving her any trouble, but she said she could not drive that far, so it would fall to me to do the driving. Both Theresa and I frowned on this idea because we would be up late the night before and maybe having a few drinks while there. We were both really sad about this 'cause we really wanted to go. We tried every way we could think of. Finally, Theresa looks at me with that grin on her face and says, "Let's take a limo." I started laughing. I laughed so hard I thought I would have a slight accident. I told her, "You're serious, aren't you?" She looked at me and said yes. She made me laugh. I told her, "Hey, it could happen. What's the worst that could happen? I call a couple of them and find out their price, and if it's too much, just tell them, we can't afford that much. Are they going to kill me? No, so they hang up." She said, "Go ahead and see what you can find out. Like you say, they can't kill you over the phone." So I got the phone book and started looking up some numbers.

We decided that we would try the one we had used when we went to Boston to catch a plane to Ireland and maybe one or two more. Sounded like the beginning of a plan to me, so I started calling.

Well, the first one didn't answer; they had their answering machine on, so I left my name and number. Then, I tried the next one; they had an answering service answer, so I left our name and number again. You know how everyone always says the third time is the charm? They lie.

Later I tried again. Someone answered the phone. He had a Middle-eastern accent, and I have a Southern accent, so we both had to deal with a different accent. It turned out to be the owner of the limo service. I told him what we wanted, and he said he would have to figure it out and call me back. He would have to see how many miles it was from there to here. So I gave him Theresa's number and told him that we would be waiting to hear from him.

Helen said she was going to leave and go home. We asked if she didn't want to stay for supper, but she said no. So we told her good-bye and walked her to the door. We then decided to eat something, so we started to fix a salad and broil some fish. We seem to enjoy the same type of food. We would love to be able to eat anything, but our age and our weight tell us that we must be prudent about what we indulge in.

After eating and doing the dishes, we decide to get on the computer and go into the chat room and talk to our buddies. When we went into the chat room, we let everyone know that I had arrived safely. They wanted to know if it was snowing. We were happy to tell them that it hadn't snowed since last night. We got the weather report from all around from everyone. Jersey was cold and snowy; in fact, the eastern United States was cold and snowy in some spots. So we knew that we would be getting it tomorrow. We didn't need to go anywhere till Helen's birthday anywhere. Then if we had to, we could have something brought in. We talked to our friends for a while; then we signed off. We were going to the store, in case, we got snowed in. Wal-Mart was only a few blocks away, so we didn't have far to go. We found everything we needed and a bunch of stuff that we didn't need. It didn't take us long to do all of that, and we were back at Theresa's within an hour.

After we put everything away the phone started. Every time that we hung it up, it started again. We were about ready to quit answering it when the guy from the limo service called. He and I exchanged pleasantries, and then he got down to business. He repeated what we wanted to make sure that he had it right. He did. The limo would pick us up at 6:00 a.m., then drive us to the Willows in Dunellen, New Jersey, wait for us while we had lunch with our friends, and then return us back to Theresa's home. Yes, I agreed; this is what we wanted. Then he hit me with a price. I asked if the tip was included. He told me, "No, but he could add it." So I told him that I wanted him to add it. So he did, and then, he gave me the price. I wrote it down on a piece of paper, so I could show it to Theresa. She looked at it and then asked me, "Are you sure you heard him right? I know he has an accent, check and make sure that is what he said." So I said to him, "Would you tell me the price again? I want to make sure I heard you correctly." So he told me the same thing again. So I asked him to tell Theresa what he had just quoted me. He was happy to do so. When he told her the same thing I had written on the paper, she started doing a little jig. I asked him to hold on for a second, and then Theresa and I discussed it. It was a big yes between the two of us; we could swing it. It was great. I told him that we thought it would work, and I reminded him that there would be three of us going. He said this was fine, no problem. He already had all the information that he would need, so he confirmed it with me.

We were so thrilled we could not believe that this was going to work. We were going to see all of our friends Sunday, March 17, St Patrick's Day, around 1:00 p.m., have lunch, talk as much as we could till they threw us out, and then be driven back to Maine. This was great, and we could afford it. We were so happy that when Helen came over we told her that she was going to New Jersey on St. Patrick's Day. She told us she couldn't afford it. We told her she didn't have to, that we had taken care of everything. She got so excited that she started laughing and crying, and doing the jig. We all ended up doing the jig.

Two days later, Theresa called her sister, Helen, and her niece Tina and her daughter, Helen, and invited all of them to go out for supper. They all agreed. They all thought we were going to celebrate the other's birthday. We didn't tell them we were going to celebrate all of them. When they all got to Theresa's, we said, "Where's the best place for Chinese food?" They all decided on the same place, so that is where we took off to.

When we got in the restaurant, Theresa pulled the owner to the side while the waitress lead the rest of us to a table. She gave me a wink when she joined us. This meant that she had told the owner that we had three birthdays to celebrate with these ladies, and we needed something special for dessert. He told her to let him take care of it, and we would really be surprised. So, she left it to him.

We all ordered. It looks like we all ordered different things. That was good; we could sample if we wanted to. We had a grand time kidding around with the birthday girls. The waitress came to clear a place on the table and to take away what she could. She did a good job; she had left a place in the middle. Then, I saw the owner coming with a dish that he was holding high. The dish was smoking; it had three candles on it.

You could never believe the wonderful cake we got. It was watermelon on the sides, and in the middle were cut-up pineapples, oranges, with cherries, and a candle sticking out of it. There were three. It had other kinds of fruit around the outside of it. It was beautiful; everyone in the place wanted to take a picture of it. We sang "Happy Birthday" to all three, and everyone in the place joined in. Then we devoured the cake. What a wonderful end to a great day. The three birthday girls were in tears, and Theresa and I were laughing. It was great. When we left the restaurant to go back to Theresa's, it had started snowing. We were not worried; we didn't need to go back out till Saturday night for the Irish American dance. That was three days away.

By the middle of the next morning, it had stopped snowing, but they promised that it would snow again that night. I had a great idea. Well, I thought it was a great idea. I wanted to rent some minks and gowns and jewelry for us to go to New Jersey in. Theresa thought I had lost my mind. I told her, "We should dress up to meet our friends. You know what they say about first impressions, and this would be the first time we would see them. Since we were going in a limo, we should play it to the full tilt." What a St. Patrick's Day that would be. Needless to say, when she called Helen and told her, together they shot my idea down. What a bummer! Can't have any fun around here! What we did instead was go to the party store and get some St. Patty's stuff to wear. We got head pieces with "Happy St. Patrick's Day" on it, some green leis for around our necks, and some garters with "Happy St. Patrick's Day" on them. We got a few other things to go with it too. We would be ready for Saturday night and Sunday. I still thought my idea was better.

Well, needless to say, it snowed till Friday night. Saturday, some of the snow melted. We were glad to see that because we were meeting Helen and her girlfriend for the dinner dance. Theresa felt all right about driving to the Irish American club. We did nothing but lull around and get ready to go out at 5:30 p.m. It started at 6:00 p.m.

Helen-Tina-Helen's birthday cake

Portland irish dancers

When we got into the car, there was some scattered snow on the ground, but it was not bad. We had no problem getting to the club. We got down and went into the hall. There was hardly anyone there, but Theresa knew everyone, and they all spoke with her; she introduced me to all. The tables were set up beautifully. The band was still setting up. I hadn't realized that there would be a band there too. They gave us a slip of paper for the door prize, and then we went to our table. We went to the table, and before we knew it, Helen and her girlfriend were there. It looked like there was a stream of people still coming in the door. The waitresses were bringing our food to the tables and a man was announcing on the mike for us to go ahead and eat. He said the dancers would perform after we were finished. Well, we had already gotten a drink and told Helen and Betty to order one for them and another for us. The chicken was fine, and we all enjoyed our food and drinks. When we finished, the Irish dancers performed. They were great. They really were in sync. The costumes were fantastic. (As a mother who had made eighteen years of dance costumes for her daughter and others, I could appreciate all the work that went into them.) We enjoyed them immensely.

Next, they decided to give out the door prizes. They had six of them. Wow! So they called the first number, and you will never guess who it was. Me! Can you imagine me, who was from the bayou country, who was visiting, but was of Irish heritage? Naturally, they asked my name and where I was from. I think I was the only foreigner there. Hehehe!

Everyone got a big laugh out of this. They gave me a wonderful tape of Irish music. After this, they called the next number, guess who? Yep! It was Theresa. Well, the whole place went up in a roar. It was so funny.

The two of us had taken the first two prizes. If the next number called was either Helen or Betty, I was going to make a dash for the door. After all the door prizes were given, the band started, and the dancing began. We had a great time. Helen got on the floor to show me the steps to one of the dances, and everyone stopped dancing and watched her. When she finished, they all clapped. She was embarrassed, but she did it so good. Before we knew it, it was 1:00 a.m. We needed to leave because the limo would be there to pick us up at 6:00 a.m. So we went home and to sleep. Helen assured us that she would be at Theresa's for 6:00 a.m.

At 5:15 a.m., we were up and getting ready to go. I was downing coffee, trying to open my eyes. Theresa was getting dressed. After she finished in the bathroom, I went in and got ready. We were both ready for 5:45. We are good. We gathered up all the stuff we had to bring, including something to nibble on and four ham sandwiches. We knew we would be hungry by the time we got there.

Helen arrived at six o'clock, and the limo was right behind her. We were aware that our driver would be a woman, but when Reggie stepped out of the limo, we were pleased. She had a chauffer's uniform on, and she was a tall blonde. She took some of the stuff we were bringing to the limo.

We were walking to the limo when Reggie opened the doors for us. Wow! This was nice. We did good. Reggie told us, "Good morning, ladies. My name is Reggie, and I will be you driver." She checked our destination with us to make sure she had the correct information. Then she told us if we needed anything, she would be happy to get it for us. She told us there was bottled water and soft drinks in the fridge and to help ourselves. We had brought our own water, along with a bag of goodies. We did not know that all that is provided for you in the limo. Helen asked her, "How long do you think it will take us to get to the restaurant?" Reggie told her between six to eight hours, depending on the traffic going through New York, but she didn't think it would be too bad because it was Sunday morning, and she didn't think that it would be bad when we went through.

We all thought we would be able to take a nap on the way. That didn't happen. We guessed the few hours we had slept already and our anxiety of going kept us awake. So we talked all the way there. Theresa told Reggie the last limo ride we took was when we returned from Ireland to Boston. She asked us a few questions about Ireland and that was all Peggy needed to start. She told her all about our Ireland trip and had her laughing as well as the rest of us.

When we got to New York, we were glad that Reggie was driving and not us. She had no problem. She knew which exits to take and which way to go so she would be in all the right lanes. We marveled at how easily she did it. After we got on the Jersey side, we stopped for a break. Our legs needed stretching, and a few other things needed attention. It was about a thirty-minute stop. When we got out of the limo, people were stretching their necks to see who was in the limo. We disappointed them. We weren't famous.

We returned to the limo, and we were off again. We would be there soon, we hoped. Peggy still wished that they would have dressed to the nines. She was still happy that they were going like they were too. When we got to Dunellen, it started to snow. Boy, we didn't need that today.

Reggie drove right to the Willows. She had very good directions. It was a few minutes after twelve, so we had Reggie drive us around back so we could relax and walk a little. The group's reservation was not till 1:00 p.m.

We asked Reggie what she would do while we were meeting with our friends. She told us that she would check in with her office and then lie down on the seat and take a nap. Helen asked her if she would get something to eat. She told her yes when she was calling her office.

It had stopped snowing, so we got out of the limo to walk a little. When we got back in the limo, Reggie asked us if we wanted her to drive us to the front door. We were in the back parking lot so we told her yes. We started to put on our St. Patrick's Day stuff when someone knocked on the window next to Helen. She jumped almost out of her skin, and when she saw who it was, she had that door open in seconds.

It was one of our buddies, Don. He wanted to know what we were doing there. He said that he understood that we would not be able to make it because of the dance last night. We all laughed and told him that it's a woman's prerogative to change her mind. He laughed. He was one of the few men in the chat room with us. It was good to see him. We talked for a few minutes, and then it was time for us to go into the restaurant to meet the rest of the group. So Don told us he would see us inside. Reggie drove us to the front door, and we got out.

When we got inside, all of the group was surprised. They just couldn't believe that we had taken a limo from Maine to eat lunch with them in New Jersey. Then we all started talking at the same time. Soon, the waitress came to take our order, and none of us were ready. We hadn't even looked at the menu. We all opened our menu and started to order. As soon as we had done that we went back to talking. Peggy said, "It's time for picture taking. So she started taking photos of all of us. Helen, Theresa, and Peggy had on the St. Patty's Day stuff, and they were handing out the leis for the others to wear. The restaurant had St. Patty's Day decorations on the walls, so we blended right in. Peggy wanted someone to take her picture of her sexy knees with the St. Patty's Day garter on them. This is a thing with her; she always says the best part of her body is her knees 'cause they are sexy. Well, Don took the picture, and she was happy then. The food arrived, and we all started to eat. The next few hours flew by. That's what happens when you are having fun. It was so nice. We could now say that we had met some more of our chat friends.

Susantru, Helen, Don's hands. Peppi, Theresa, Edschool
This is one of the pictures that was taken. I don't know what happened to Don. We can see his hands next to Helen even if we can't see his face.

As we were ready to leave, Reggie drove around to the front door to pick us up. All our friends were flabbergasted. They could not believe what we had done to get to their dinner. The people in the restaurant were rubbernecking because our friends were taking pictures.

We got in the car and headed back to Maine. We knew we had a long ride, but we didn't mind. We had found a way to be with our friends. What a day. We could have not asked for better. We wished that the ones who couldn't make it would have been able to be there.

With Reggie at the wheel, we relaxed and dozed off. When we got to New York, Reggie told us, "Look at the lights from the Twin Towers." There they were in all their glory. For the whole world to see. We will never forget. It was an awe-inspiring sight. The perfect finish to a wonderful day. A day none of us would forget. We talked about it for a while, and then we dozed back off. We stopped one time on the way back to take care of things that needed our attention. Reggie was a great driver, and it was a smooth ride.

When we got back to Theresa's, it was almost midnight. Peggy paid Reggie, and Helen got into her car to go home. She told us she would call in the morning. We went into Theresa's and fell into the beds.

The next morning was kind of lost to us. We slept late and just lay around. Good thing I wasn't leaving today. We were worn-out from our weekend. Tomorrow was another day. The day of my departure, but still we had today.

When we got up, we had our coffee, and tea, and our breakfast, and got dressed. I started to pack my suitcases. We still had about 3 hours before I had to leave. So what did we do? We got on the Internet to see if any of our buddies were on there. We had yet to tell them of our limo ride, and we wanted to share that with them.

Yep, you guessed it, they already knew. Our dinner companions had already shared the news with them. Joanne said she could not think of how we did it, and that she would have never thought of it. I told her that Theresa had the brain storm on that one. (They always blame me for the crazy antics.) Of course, I went along with it, and helped. The end result was great. We were proud of our Limo ride. We had accomplished what we had set out to do. Isn't that what life is all about? Just think, if we had given up on our meeting these wonderful people, we would have not met them. That would have been a tragedy. One that neither of us could accept very easily.

Well, it was time for us to leave for the airport. We got off the Internet, and shut down the computer. Put on our coats and scarves, and wheeled the luggage to the car.

The ride to the airport was pretty quiet, had it not been for the Irish music we had playing, it would have been very dull. We dreaded saying goodbye to each other. We had formed a special kind of friendship, that day long ago, on the Internet. One that has lasted a long time, with more joy than we can say and anticipation of the day to come.

Bye, see you next trip.

Theresa and Peggy

Maine Trip

The phone was ringing. It seemed like every time Theresa got started doing her housework today, the phone would ring. She went to her desk and answered it.

"Hey, lady, you busy?" It was Peggy. "Not too busy to talk to you." she said. "Well, then would you please go open your door?" Theresa asked, "Why am I opening my door?" "To let me in so we can talk and have a cup of tea," she replied. Theresa opened the door, and there stood Peggy. She was taken aback to see her here. She was supposed to be in Philadelphia, clearing up some stuff from her father's estate.

"What are you doing here? Why didn't you call? I could have picked you up at the airport," she said. "I didn't fly, I came on the train," Peggy said. "Anyway, Dad's attorney is stuck on a trial case that won't finish for a week to ten days, so instead of staying at Aunt Dot's and having nothing to do, I decide to pay you a visit. When he is finished with his case, his secretary is going to call me here, and I will take a flight back or go by train, depending on how much time I have, and finish up everything." "This is great, now I can show you Maine. I have always wanted to do that," said Theresa. "That sounds great, and I can visit my cousin John while I am here."

We fixed tea, and Theresa had some tea cakes that were great with tea, so we sat down and indulged. We decided that we would start in the morning and see where the road lead us.

We started out going south toward Kennebunkport. This was something that Peggy really wanted to see. The summer home of former President George Bush, Sr. After seeing that, we started for the town, which is well known for antique shops and art galleries. Peggy loves antiques, so we had to go into several stores and look. She loved some of the things, but they were a little too pricey for her. We took the shore road, which is the scenic route that boarders the beautiful Atlantic Ocean. It was magnificent. We stopped at another town named Old Orchard. This town is well known for an amusement pier and boardwalk. It also has five miles of sandy beaches. We spent a few hours just looking and taking pictures. After that we were tired, so we head for home.

Portland, Me Lighthouse

Portland, Me Fort

Portland, Me Gazebo

The next day, we went to Two Lights. This is where their foghorn is located. It also has a park and two lighthouses. Theresa was telling Peggy that when she was very young, she used to go there and pick periwinkles. During World War II, many German subs were sighted here. It has been a known fact that one of the subs sank one of our warships near here.

Staying on the shore road, we stopped to visit Portland Head Light. This is one of the most notorious and photographed lighthouses in Maine. It is known as Fort Williams. Next, we went to Fort Preble; this is where many servicemen were stationed during the war. A little south of that was the largest shipyard in the state.

Theresa decided that we had enough of the shore, so she drove inland. They have many lakes and mountains. One of the largest lakes is named Sebago. In places of that lake, the depth is 316 feet, and also, it is 49 feet below sea level. One end of the lake is a town named Naples.

We met Theresa's daughter Mary and her sister, Helen, there for lunch. After lunch, we decided to take the tour on the cruise ship. The *River Queen* is a replica of the famed Mississippi River stern paddle wheelers. Unfortunately, the water was too rough for the trip, they cancelled it.

On the way back to the house, Theresa thought Peggy would like to see Freeport. Many tourists visit this town because of the famous store that is there. L. L. Bean is noted for their camping and clothing materials. Peggy has a son that loves to go hunting, and she loves materials; she is always sewing something, so Theresa thought this would be a good stop. It was. Peggy loved all the materials she saw and even bought a few. (She was going to have to ship them Parcel Post to her home because she didn't have much room in the suitcase she had brought.) Then, she looked at the hunting equipment that they had and was so impressed she called her son to see if he wanted anything there. It turned out that the store shipped all of her purchases for her.

South of there is the famous DeLorme Map Store. As we entered the building, we saw a huge globe named Eartha. It is as tall as a three-story building. It showed all over the world. It was very impressive, and Peggy was glad that they had stopped there.

We decided to return home; we were both a little tired, and tomorrow was another day.

Theresa's daughter Helen and niece Tina were coming by to visit, and they were bringing supper with them. This was much appreciated by us because our feet were killing us from all the walking we did today.

After dinner, we decided to play a game of cards. We laughed at Peggy; she had never played this game before, and she vowed she never would again. It was cribbage!

We had a great time, but the evening was ending too soon. Theresa and Peggy had planned to do more sightseeing tomorrow. So they called it an early evening.

We decided to go to Portland and take the *Duck* Tour. The *Duck* is an authentic WWII amphibious landing vehicle. We boarded the *Duck* at the Old Port. Portland's old port had been restored to a nineteenth-century splendor with cobblestone streets and Victorian brick building. Most of Portland's best attractions are within walking distance. The Portland Museum of Art, housing a permanent collection of Picasso, Winslow Homer, Renoir, Degas, Monet, and other masters. It was amazing. Peggy had never seen this many of the master's painting all together. She was awestruck. She kept telling Theresa, "Look at this. Look at this. Look at this." Next door to the museum is the Children's Museum. Nearby, there is a Victorian mansion, one of the best examples of Italianate architecture in the country. We also visited the famed poet, Henry Wadsworth Longfellow's childhood home, with the original furniture and beautiful restored gardens nearby.

We were invited to Theresa's friend Jean's place. She has a condo overlooking Casco Bay. This particular day, there was a large cruise ship in port. They told Peggy that the largest cruise ship that was docked there was the *Queen Mary 2*. We waited till the ship departed from the pier. The fireboat with its red, white, and blue water streamers and many small boats were near the ship as it left the bay. It was a beautiful sight to see. Portland has been having a resurgence of cruise ships lately. It helps with the economy.

We decided to go eat at the famous DiMillo's Floating Restaurant. We had a great meal, especially their famous lobster dinners. It was delicious. We left soon after dinner; we had plans for tomorrow.

Today, we are supposed to meet Peggy's cousin John for lunch in Augusta. Peg was anxious to go; she hadn't seen John in a long time. An hour before, they were supposed to leave, it started snowing heavy. They hoped that it would stop, but fate was not shining in our corner this morning. Peggy called John and cancelled our lunch. She was very disappointed that she could not introduce John to Theresa. Theresa had already met and stayed with his mother and father in Florida, Jack and Ginny. The rest of the day was glum. There wasn't much to do but read. In the afternoon, Peggy attorney's secretary called and said the attorney would be able to see her in two days. This gave her enough time to travel back to Philadelphia tomorrow at her aunt's home. Then, the next day, she could finish up her dad's estate and go home to Louisiana. We had a grand time on this little side trip of Peggy's.

Theresa was sorry that she had to leave but was glad that they had a few days together that were unplanned and she got to show Peggy her wonderful state.

Well, we will see you next time. Bye.

Peggy and Theresa

Our Intentions

When we started thinking of our tours, we thought we could see most of our friends in the senior chat room. As it turns out, due to our poor health and age, we did not get to see them all.

We were going to visit Paula in New Hampshire, Pharm in New Jersey, Joan in Ohio, June in Illinois, Loretta in Indiana, Winn in Tennessee, and Frank in Alabama. We are sorry that we didn't see them all.

At this time, we also would like to acknowledge our deceased friends that used to be in our room: Susan, Smokey, Ummses, Happy Irishman, Mary, Misty, Mary Jo, Txnobody, Stu, Molly, Dirkie, and Mudman.

We would like to thank our family and friends who helped us with this book.

Our thanks and prayers are with all of you.

Margaret and Theresa

CPSIA information can be obtained
at www.ICGtesting.com
Printed in the USA
BVOW06s2148271216
471993BV00001B/16/P

9 781465 391766